Linda Schreurs is [illegible] messengers who speaks with a prophetic edge to the church, God's bride, about preparing the way for His coming, to be ready and properly adorned for her Heavenly Husband. Linda is also like a twenty-first century scribe who has over the years watched, prayed, and documented what she has heard in the secret place of His presence and seen with a discerning eye in our land. As you read *Armageddon Bride*, you will hear the Spirit say, "Come into a closer revelatory relationship with the Lord and take courage to live the life of the knowledge of Him."

—Rev. Pat Chen
Founder and President
First Love Ministries International
San Ramon, California
The Secret Place Prayer Room
Washington, DC

The Battle of the Ages and the battle for a spotless bride is raging in our culture like never before! It is a battle for passions: the unbridled passion of darkness and the fiery passion for Jesus. Linda is a standard-bearer of truth, using the Word of God as a two-edged sword to divide between the thoughts and intentions of the reader's heart and yet writing in such a manner that a deep longing pierces your heart to love Him more! Linda is raising a moral and spiritual standard, challenging the body of Christ to higher levels of conscience and accountability so the bride is spotless and without wrinkle, ready to meet her Bridegroom!

Armageddon Bride is a divine plumb line for the body of Christ, bringing in a fresh new fear of the Lord that has been lost or weakened! It is a trumpet blast that definitely "rocks the boat" of compromise! Her message is so needed today, due to the perversion and moral failures of leaders within the church and the world. Yet, in reading it, your heart becomes awakened as it cries out for a deeper intimacy with Jesus.

—Jill Austin
Founder and President
Master Potter Ministries
Author and conference speaker

This book is one of those deep things God has brought about. Linda has exquisitely captured the Mother heart of God that would go to war for her children. What captivated me so much in her chapters was that we, the Bride of Christ as a whole, are called to go to war against injustice. And this war is neither by might nor by power, but by His Spirit. What spirit might that be? God's Holy Spirit is the opposite of the spirit of hate, fear, injustice, and oppression that rules our world. It is only His great love that can dispel the darkness of hate and fear.

We in India are faced with the same problems that plague all developing nations. The rich get richer and the poor get poorer; injustice multiplies itself endlessly. How can this be stopped? How is it possible for a pattern followed for hundreds of generations to ever be changed? How can an entire people group ever know that they were made to rule and not be ruled? How can they know unless someone tells them? I highly recommend that every disciple of Christ reads this book for the answers.

—Shampa Rice
Director, Iris India

Linda Schreurs embodies in her life the very noble things written in this book: passion for Jesus, nobility of character and wisdom, and faithfulness and integrity in her family and marriage. As an intercessor and worshiper she brings an urgency of end-time responsiveness to God and a fragrance of the glory of Christ in these troubled days. Read, be stirred, and be refreshed.

—Lou Engle

Linda Schreurs, in her newest book, *Armageddon Bride*, brings the latest insights from the Spirit, soundly founded on the Scriptures, to meet the need in these crisis days. Linda's book is the most fascinating reading regarding Spirit-anointed thoughts on Armageddon. Read it today.

—Don H. Polston, PhD
Author of *Winning Through Faith Imaging*

ARMAGEDDON B·R·I·D·E

LINDA SCHREURS

ARMAGEDDON BRIDE by Linda Schreurs
Published by Creation House
A Strang Company
600 Rinehart Road
Lake Mary, Florida 32746
www.creationhouse.com

Author's note: the name *satan* is not capitalized that no significance be given to him.

Design Director: Bill Johnson
Cover designer: Amanda Potter

Author's photo by John N. Holtorf, Holtorf Photography, Des Moines, IA

Library of Congress Control Number: 2008923823
International Standard Book Number: 978-1-59979-375-7

08 09 10 11 12 — 98765432
Printed in the United States of America

I passionately dedicate this book to our Lord Jesus Christ, our heavenly Bridegroom. He spoke to the core of my being, laying its message upon my surrendered heart. It's His book and He deserves all praise and glory!

Secondly, I devotedly dedicate this book to my parents, Gunner and Dellrose Jakobsen. Your lives have spoken volumes to the value of a godly, loving, committed marriage and the bond of family unity. I love you!

Thirdly, I lovingly dedicate this book to the most endearing man in my life, my husband, Michael. And also to our three children, Celine, Sarah, and Claire. You are all the greatest gift God has ever given me!

Finally, I gratefully dedicate this book to my core intercessors who prayed diligently for the birthing of this book. Thank you!

CONTENTS

Introduction.....1

Prologue.....5

1 A Passionate Pursuit.....11

2 The Dawning of Divine Romance.....19

3 The Envy of the Enemy.....29

4 Winning Back the Bride.....37

5 Compromise—A Lukewarm Dish.....49

6 Identity Crisis.....57

7 Persecution.....69

8 Confusion.....83

9 Destruction or Discernment? Blood Donor?.....93

10 God's Word, A Hot Commodity.....107

11 False Shepherds.....119

12 Intimacy With God.....139

13 Code of Conduct.....151

14 The Romance of Israel.....163

15 Battleground.....177

16 The Engraved Wedding Invitation.....189

17 Prophetic Bridal Showers.....201

18 The Wedding.....211

Epilogue.....223

Notes.....227

INTRODUCTION

A HUGE, FIERY, GOLDEN writing pen was suspended in midair right in front of me. As I gazed upon this strange phenomenon with my spirit eyes I stopped breathing, momentarily gasping in awe and wonder. "What *is* this?" I wondered to myself. Then, quite suddenly, my heart could not hold back speaking forth the spiritual vision before me. Words from my mouth unfolded in front of the people gathered together for prayer, and I was compelled to declare the pen's presence in the room. The other people in the room stood still as they soaked in the astounding presence of the Lord, and wondered what this vision meant.

The tearing of the thin membrane separating the natural realm from the spiritual realm on that peculiar, beautiful night in October 2006 was extremely significant! The revelatory and prophetic declarations spoken came by way of the Holy Spirit who opened up the heavens before us. This was the Lord's unique way of assuring us that we all have a divine destiny to fulfill. That destiny has been written in His Book of Life with the blood of Calvary's cross and through the fire of the Holy Spirit.

Do you know your destiny? If not, why not? And if you do, are you walking in it? Or, could you be erasing it by not living for the One who created you, died for your sins, and paid your ticket to glory?

The world is changing quickly. Time is of the essence, and we need to walk out the divine destiny God has laid out for us since before the foundation of the earth. It is now or never!

My vision of the golden pen was the Lord's spectacularly creative method of capturing my attention to affirm and confirm the divine assignment He gave me for this book you now hold in your hands. It has been commissioned by His grace, love, and mercy for a prophetic end-times look at what we are about to face from this generation onward. Know this for certain: this time capsule we call earth is going to change dramatically, affecting every human being from every tribe, tongue, and nation. The earth will not last forever, but the kingdom of God most certainly will.

Don't just read this book, read *the Lord's book*—the Holy Bible. Find out for yourself what His God-breathed scriptures have to say about your life in the natural and in the supernatural: "Heaven and earth will pass away, but My Words will not pass away" (Matt. 25:35). Get ready! Everything is about to change!

> My tongue is the pen of a ready writer.
>
> —Psalm 45:1

> Then the Lord answered me and said, 'Record the vision and inscribe it on tablets; that the one who reads it may run. For the vision is yet for the appointed time; it hastens toward the goal, and it will not fail. Though it tarries, wait for it; for it will certainly come, it will not delay.
>
> —Habakkuk 2:2–3

Suddenly the fingers of a man's hand emerged and began writing opposite the lamp stand on the plaster of the wall of the kings palace, and the king saw the back of the hand that did the writing. Then the king's face grew pale, and his thoughts alarmed him; and his hip joints went slack, and his knees began knocking together.". . . . "But the God in whose hand are your life-breath and your ways, you have not glorified. Then the hand was sent from Him, and this inscription was written out. 'Now this is the inscription that was written out: 'Mene, Mene, Tekel, Upharsin.' This is the interpretation of the message: 'Mene'—God has numbered your kingdom and put an end to it. 'Tekel'—you have been weighed on the scales and found deficient. 'Peres'—your kingdom has been divided and given over to the Medes and Persians.'

—Daniel 5:5–6, 23–28

For truly I say to you, 'until heaven and earth pass away, not the smallest letter or stroke shall pass away from the Law, until all is accomplished.'

—Matthew 5:18

PROLOGUE

INTERCEPTIONS BY THE Holy Spirit on man's playing field of life are extraordinary defining moments such as the one described in the Introduction of this book. You simply can never forget them!

An ordinary day can become extraordinary and change your life forever. This has happened to me a number of times. One such occurrence was a typical Sunday afternoon several years ago.

The rather windy and cloudy day wasn't notable until my eyes caught sight of the dark clouds that began swirling and mingling rapidly overhead. They ran a striking contrast to the big, white fluffy ones. The skies turned dark, as the clouds seemed to wage war over one another as to who would dominate the heavens. "I wonder if a storm is brewing?" I thought to myself. Settling down in a comfortable chair, I threw my feet up on the footstool and began scanning the Sunday newspaper, reading nothing in particular.

Suddenly and without any warning, an odd and overwhelming sense of sorrow sweeps over me. Alarmingly, I hear battle sounds! War! Sounds of war! How close is it? Am I in danger? How will I fight? Who's in this battle? Who is the enemy? What is the reason for the attack? Why does it feel so intense? What can this be? Why do I feel such a sense of foreboding? What is going on? How can this be? This is something we've never experienced! I'm in my own home, who could be intruding? I'm not in Iraq. I'm not in Afghanistan. I'm sitting in my own home in middle America minding my own business. But extreme danger is lurking nearby!

I hear such intense clashing that I cannot control my sudden and deep sobs. My husband, glancing in my direction, knows something is going on. He does not scold or mock me, but begins to pray. He knows I am having a prophetic experience that is as real as the back of my hand.

He Who Has an Ear

The Lord has an admonition from the opening chapters of the Book of Revelation, "He who has an *ear*, let him hear what the Spirit says to the churches" (Rev. 2:7, 11, 17, 29; 3:6, 13, 22). I was definitely hearing something powerful that day.

Most of us have heard either by radio or television this interruptive phrase, "This is a test. For the next thirty seconds, this station will conduct a test of the Emergency Broadcast System. This is only a test." On that peculiar Sunday afternoon in the spring of the year, there was no such warning device in the natural realm other than those strange clouds. If we would only note God's words in 1 Corinthians 15:46 that the natural precedes the spiritual, we might better ascertain the times in which we live. Also read 2 Samuel 11:1, "Then it happened in the spring at the time when kings go out to battle."

There was only one agent who alerted me to this impending battle, the Holy Spirit, "And I saw heaven opened; and behold, a white horse, and He who sat upon it is called Faithful and True; and in righteousness He judges and *wages war*" (Rev. 19:11, emphasis added).

I heard all this in my spirit. It was as plain as day because the spiritual realm is as real, and even more so, than the natural realm in which we live and move. (See Acts 17:28.) We are made of flesh and blood to be sure, but there is also a spirit within each one of us placed there by our Divine Creator, the Lord God Jehovah. Our bodies are His creativity. We have been made in His likeness with a spiritual breath that lives forever. (See Genesis 1:26.) It is He who gives us the freedom of choice if we want to live *with* Him or *without* Him in that eternal spiritual realm. You and I do not have a choice in being physically born, but it is an open book as to how our spirits will live on after death. We have the final say on that one. God forces no one into His holy dwelling place. Our names are recorded in the books of county courthouses all across America, but are they recorded in the books of the courts of heaven? (See Revelation 21:27.)

The Courts

The earthly courts and the heavenly courts are being called into session where *decisive battles* are now being fiercely waged. These battles are *not* against flesh and blood as some would suppose but, "against the rulers, against the powers, against the world forces of this darkness, against the spiritual forces of wickedness in heavenly places" (Eph. 6:12). The question is, are you and I ready for these battles? Are we armed for war? Or will we suffer from a sudden and vicious sneak attack of the enemy endangering the loss our eternal souls?

It is time we understand that every man, woman, and child is going to have to be prepared at this precarious hour for humanity's end-time saga. Life and death decisions are going to have to be made more quickly than ever before. Why? Because *time*, as we know it, is growing shorter and shorter. There is a generation of people who *will be* the final generation on the face of the earth. This will not be a movie—this will be the real deal. Everything mankind has ever known will be dramatically impacted in this epic battle of the ages. All peoples of every tribe, tongue, and nation will be affected. (See Revelation 5:9.) There will not be one person who will come out of it unscathed because it will engulf the entire globe.

LINES BEING DRAWN

It is beyond our imagination to consider the epic war of all wars. What would the war look like that combines all the ages of mankind since the foundations of the earth? It is unimaginable, unthinkable, and unfathomable, but it *is* inevitable! The battle lines are now being drawn. A holocaust of immeasurable portions is soon to be upon us. A third of mankind is going to be slaughtered. (See Revelation 9:15.) What could possibly cause such horrid devastation? I don't have all the answers, but I do know this: God the Father declares to us through His scriptures that this end-time battle is about *love.* John 3:16 says that God so *loved* the world that He gave His only begotten Son, that those who believe in Him would attain to eternal life. God's Word, Jesus Christ, wonderfully became flesh and dwelt among us. God's Son Jesus has a beautiful bride called the church and He is coming back to planet earth to take His church away to be with Him forever and ever. But there will be a fight! It will be for her purity! The Son is returning for a bride without spot or wrinkle. (See Ephesians 5:27.) The battle now rages to intensifying degrees. Is anyone listening? Does anyone even care?

A question each of us must answer is, "Whom do I choose to please—God or man?" To please God means to agree with His Word, His commands, and to live in righteousness. If we choose to live according to that which pleases man, we will find ways to excuse sin, to be temperate rather than holy, fearing the opinions of others more than we fear God.

God's church, His end-times bride, will be holy, pure, and sold out to Him. No fear of man (homophobia) will diminish that. I suggest a word for this hour—*theophobia*—a holy, reverential fear of God!

Scripture clearly states the risen Son of God, who is our Heavenly Bridegroom, Jesus, is coming to earth a second and last time to take His pure, spotless bride away to be with Him forevermore. Therefore, the earthly marital union that's being assaulted, contested, maligned, and redefined according to man's ways and not according to God's true covenant, is a major focus of this book. Gay marriage and congruently, the global issue of abortion, which seeks to destroy earthly life, reflects the battle for eternal spiritual life. We are now at the precipice of the final, epic *battle of the Ages*—Armageddon!

The book you now hold in your hands is as a fire about to be lit! It's an insight into the very intense and very heated battle about God's holy and abiding *love*. It's the love story of all the ages culminating at the closure of the earthly realm and the beginning of a heavenly one for all of eternity. It is the final saga of a torrid love affair with the lover of our soul, the Lord Jesus Christ, who is coming back to earth a second time to get His bride. He has an intense love and desire for every soul to come into communion with Him, that none should perish (2 Pet. 3:9).

The world is fast coming down to its final hour and is now having a major *identity* crisis. The question is, "Who is the true bride?"

May the Holy Spirit reveal her to you.

> And the Spirit and the bride say, 'Come.' And let the one who hears say, 'Come.' And let the one who is thirsty come; let the one who wishes take the water of life without cost.
>
> —Revelation 22:17

◆ one ◆

A PASSIONATE PURSUIT

THE PASSIONATE, HOT breath of the Almighty God has been blowing upon humanity for thousands of years. Do you feel it? Do you have a desire to know your Creator God intimately? Are you aware that He is passionately pursuing a close relationship with you? Can you reciprocate this desire in as much passion and longing as He has for you? You most certainly can!

The "I AM" God (Exod. 3:14) is seeking for us to enter deeply into His heart and has spared nothing toward that end, having given His own Son as ransom for our very soul. His Son is His Word made flesh (John 1). Jesus is that very breath made manifest.

His Word longs for a people, a global body of believers, who are called the *church* to love Him with every fiber of their being. This body is called the Bride of Christ and He is coming back to get her! He wants her to prepare by being bathed in the hot oil of His presence. He desires her to be drenched in the power of a pure life reflecting His glory by being holy as He is holy (Lev. 11:45). He is after those who want to know Him in holy, spiritual intimacy as did John the beloved who longed to know every heartbeat, every breath, and every divine command of the Holy Shepherd (John 13:23–25).

Our heavenly Bridegroom Jesus is still looking for those who would be like King David, who was a man after God's own heart (Acts 13:22). Can this be said of us? To what extent are we pursuing God's heart? How *far* are we willing to go? Our Lord is looking for the ones who are willing to give their all for Him, being faithful and true even unto death (Rev. 2:10). Just as Jesus laid His life down for His bride, so too must she be prepared to lay her life down for Him. Upon the face of the earth, there is no greater love than this—so says His Word in John 15:13.

This is not a hard task God asks of us. Lovers are passionate, and lovers are givers. So where are those kinds of lovers who are sold out completely to Him, even if it costs them everything, perhaps even their own lives? Where are they? Who are they? Are we one of them?

The Son of God is looking for souls who will not compromise His Word, but take it as His breath decreed it. He is after those who will not give themselves to a wishy-washy, weak, watered-down Christianity that has a form, a style, or an appearance of godliness, but lacks His very nature and power. He desires those who will not abort the power and anointing of God contained in His unchangeable, eternal Word, the Bible.

A Holy Gaze

The breath of God is a fire of love pulsating through all the ages of mankind. His eyes continually go to and fro across the earth looking for those who want Him. Are you aware of this? Are you aware that this magnificent King of glory is searching for you and me so that we might know a life of pure joy beyond all measure? What immense and amazing love this is that causes the Lover of our souls to seek after those who want to know His heart intimately. What a joy to hear His breath declare it in 2 Chronicles 16:9, "For the eyes of the Lord move to and fro throughout the earth that He may strongly support those whose heart is completely His." Therefore, those fiery souls involved in this profound love with Him can gaze for hours into the expanse of the King's eyes and in unison with the angels cry: "Holy! Holy! Holy!" (Rev. 4 and 5). It is somewhat of a mystery for humanity and almost unfathomable to think that this holy God wants us to seek Him face to face!

People, listen! We have now entered a critical time where it is essential we possess a holy, reverential fear of the Almighty Jehovah God because He is the eternal epitome of power, holiness, glory, majesty, and splendor beyond all comparison or comprehension. Spiritually intimate lovers of God's heart will desire the sound of His voice above all others. This will cause them to know the sound of the trumpet at the end of the age signaling His return (Rev. 1:10). Oh, the beauty and magnificence of His face and eyes! Oh, the depth of glory found there! He declares to His one and only bride, the church, in the Old Testament book Song of Songs, "How beautiful you are! Your eyes are like doves" (1:15). The trumpet is about to sound. We must fix our gaze upon Him or risk losing eternity. It's now or never. Time is of the essence!

Lukewarmness Causes Vomit

Our Bridegroom Jesus is seeking for those who desire to know His heart above all things, not selling short for any amount of pleasure that comes from the things of this world. The lukewarmness and half-heartedness that have settled upon many of God's people have become a stagnant stench in His nostrils (Amos 4:8–12). Many live half-committed, compromised lifestyles and have become as whitewashed tombs. They "clean up well" on the outside, but on the inside they are as dead man's bones causing a spiritual, deathly stench (Matt. 23:27). God desires to put His holy breath on those dead bones once again for full and abundant life (Ezek. 37; John 10:10)!

So—how is your life going these days?
Is it abundant and full?
Or is it lacking and empty?

Consider as well those who have a nice, comfortable *form* of religion and godliness, but lack any real power to overcome the world, the flesh, and the devil (2 Tim. 3). They become losers in many areas of their lives, always wondering what's wrong. They have itchy ears wanting only to hear what makes them feel good and what will confirm their wanton lifestyles and pleasures. They do not have a fiery bone in their body, nor any true desire to know God up close and personal. They do not long to know His righteousness, holiness, purity, and divine authority. Consequently, they are living in extreme danger spiritually because the Lord is about to vomit them from His mouth (Rev. 3:16)! They may not even have enough time before their death to dial up a spiritual 9-1-1 call to the Lord who could save their soul!

Revelation 3:16 implies it is all or nothing—it's hot or not. There must be *passion* in God's people! There is nothing worse than love grown cold. But this is exactly what Jesus said would happen at the end of time (Matt. 24:12). Beware. Are you hot for God? Are you on fire for Him? Are you *passionately* pursuing Him?

Our God is a jealous God (Exod. 20:5). He will not tolerate coldness of heart, so it is imperative we wake up to the fact that neither does He tolerate lukewarmness. That is a state of Christianity putting us in critical condition and in danger of being spewed from the mouth of a holy God (Rev. 3:16). Instead of experiencing the kisses of His mouth (Deut. 30:14; Song of Songs 1:2) as He desires for us, we become as a foul stench to Him, like that of vomit—it's disgusting! Transfer that to how our lukewarm hearts must look to the Lover of our souls who gave His own life that we might know Him behind the veil (Luke 23:45).

Likewise, just as in an earthly, marital relationship where unfaithfulness can destroy the relationship, our heavenly Bridegroom will not tolerate other loves. Why? Because He wants our full desire to be toward Him and Him alone. He's number One. He's the *only* One. He's the *most high* One! He said to Moses on the mountain, "I am the Lord, thy God, you shall have no strange gods before Me" (Exod. 20:3). Anything in this life that takes precedence over a passionate pursuit of God, whether it's your career, sports, hobbies, entertainment, real estate, kids, church, or worldly relationships—whatever—it deletes your all-out love affair with Him and is an abomination in His sight. This leaves your soul in open rebellion worthy of death and destruction forever. It's His Word, not mine! The first commandment is still the first command. God's Word is unchangeable. What He says stands forever. Let us require of ourselves to put things in their proper order, to put first things first by re-prioritizing our lives before it's done for us, which would come at a hefty price, costing the loss of our heavenly home.

The King of Glory is indeed jealous for His Bride. This holy jealousy causes Him to want all of her heart and nothing less will do. This great love affair God has with His creation calls for purity. It's interesting how the great apostle Paul refers to this in 2 Corinthians 11:2, "For I am jealous for you with a godly jealousy. For I have betrothed you to one husband, that I may present you as a chaste virgin to Christ."

FIRE

The Lord is calling us to fall in love with Him either for the first time in our lives or to re-ignite our passion for Him all over again, but this time to a greater degree than anything we have known in the past. This is a new hour! He's saving the best wine for last. The bridal banquet of the ages is soon upon us (John 2).

Humanity has reached a crucible in this earthly realm. Things are changing quickly. It's evident everyday, especially in technology. You can hardly keep up with it. But that pales in comparison to the changes that are coming upon this planet to every tribe, tongue, and nation. When Jesus said He was going to come a second time, He meant it! The eternal Word of truth is ever living and interceding for us that we might not be caught unawares for the battle of the ages that is coming soon (Heb. 7:23; Rom. 8:26–27).

So where do you and I fit into this passionate pursuit of God? We need to ask ourselves, "Are we aflame with desire for the Lover of our soul and the One who died for us?" and "What's the level of our firepower?" We must recognize now more than ever that the enemy of our souls has come to snuff out any flicker or flame of love and passion we have for the Lord Jesus Christ. May our awareness now be heightened! The coming fire of God's glory will consume all things that can be shaken—the moon, the stars, the earth, and its very inhabitants (Isa. 13:13; Haggai 2:6–7, 21; Heb. 12:26). The war for the true Bride of Christ is only going to intensify as time ticks away days, weeks, months, and perhaps years, for however long the Lord of Hosts tarries before breaking the eastern sky (Matt. 24).

Purity of purpose is now on the line. Everyone must now be aware of the Armageddon Bride! The clock has now struck the final hour and the battle for the true Bride of Christ is imminent. The epic saga for the heavenly Bridegroom's intimacy with His beloved will now be proven. How will we respond?

Prayer

O Lord God Almighty, I want to find You and love You. Show me the pathway to Your divine and holy heart, that I may walk in Your presence. I desire to know the passionate flame of pursuing You with my whole heart, mind, soul, and body. I invite You to take me where I need to be. Amen.

◆ two ◆

THE DAWNING OF DIVINE ROMANCE

EVERYTHING WE HAVE ever known is about to change dramatically. A spiritual volcanic eruption will occur in the lives of people around the globe! Take heed. This is a warning! Many are slumbering at the wheel of life and are about to crash. There is a volatile shifting going on of epic proportions and it is making subtle inroads into every society. It is the battle for true identity, true love, and true intimacy. The question at this critical hour is, "Who am I?"

Do you really know who you are? Do you really know true love? It is a wonderful comfort to know true, holy, godly love. It's healing. It's deliverance. It's restoration. It's freedom. It is pure joy! You and I need it. We've simply got to have it to make it through.

This epic, Armageddon battle for the true identity of the Bride of Christ defines true love. The time capsule is about to be blown to bits, ushering in eternity. There may not even be a split-second to make that defining decision if it hasn't yet been made. In order to know beyond a shadow of a doubt who we really are, and to have the assurance that our final destiny is a good one, we need to know true love.

The Love Affair

The love affair of the ages began long ago. Who could have imagined such deep love would begin the way it did? It's almost incomprehensible, which makes it all the more intriguing and alluring. In the midst of chaos and deep darkness, how is it that love can conquer such depths? But it is this very thing that makes this story so compelling. It's God's story—and it is our story!

As the eternal Jehovah God began to design the earthly realm, it was formless and void (Gen. 1). As He breathed forth a commanding word, things began to gloriously move and shift. His voice alone created the heavens, the skies, moon and stars. He spoke into existence the mountains and all creatures microscopic and mammoth. He spoke waters of varying depths into being. The seas burst forth and little mountain streams and forest brooks began gurgling in holy array. He began adding spectacular varieties of flowers and vegetation of every imagined color and texture. Ah, the skies! They were moving with the unison of His very breath, bringing different lights in the morning and at night.

As the Almighty's commands went forth, winds blew violently, stirring, shifting, and changing the chaos of the darkness. Our Creator *spoke* a world into existence of untold majesty and splendor. How beautiful is the Divine breath! How utterly beautiful! *Ruwach! Ruwach! Ruwach* is a Hebrew word meaning, "the divine breath in motion."[1] What splendor, majesty, and glory within the mighty breath of God! There is an immense and fearsome power that is released at His every word. We would do well to listen to Him!

All those created things were truly magnificent. Nonetheless, they were not a true reflection of His glory. And so, His divine and holy breath created something entirely different than all the rest. He spoke life into a one-of-a-kind creation called a human being. He gave this being the name, *Adam.* This specially designed work of God was formed for the express purpose of knowing the divine presence up close and personal in order for the Father's nature of love and glory to be reflected back to Him as a mirror! Amazing!

Holy Design

The first specimen off the assembly line of humanity was created with a body, soul, and spirit. What joy God felt as He looked upon all He had created and declared it to be "very good!" (Gen. 1:31; 2:7). Now His reflection could be seen because God is Spirit and Adam knew Him in Spirit and in Truth (John 4:24). Adam came forth out of the will and breath of God. He loved his Maker and enjoyed the company of the Almighty. And yet, to this man, there was not found a suitable helper in tending to the joy of effortless gardening in the land of Eden. Jehovah Elohim, God of all sovereignty and power, desiring to further His own reflection of glory, gave the man a suitable helper in the holy design of something quite delightful. He decides the best fit for the man was His newest creation, a similar and yet different human being called woman. Adam found his life mate! He was elated, and like all the other created things, he had the privilege of naming her. He called her, *Eve.* Thus the team God formed out of one man and one woman—together—were a glorious crown of God's beauty.

Oh, how the Divine Creator loved them! He gave them everything! Everything one could ever imagine. Every need was met. Nothing could ever be lacking in their lives. *Labor* was an unknown word. Pain could never be felt. Beauty was in them and all around them. God was so excited! He declared all of it good! What an emotion! How often do we declare the works of God in our own lives as good?

And so it was that God the Father was full of joy as these images made in His own likeness of spirit captured His heart. The man and the woman only knew of God's pure and holy love. They were not aware of the evil lurking nearby in the dark, shadowy trees. For a long time they were simply captivated by their Creator's majestic love, as each day and each night unfurled itself in seemingly endless glory and fellowship with Him. Paradise was indeed stunningly spectacular, beautiful, and glorious.

The greatest love affair known to mankind began in the Garden of Eden as the Almighty created His shining jewel of creation—the man and the woman. The couple as ordained by God was one man and one woman. He fashioned the two of them together in an amazing configuration of unique beauty and fitness, like a synchronized puzzle of two pieces becoming one flesh in procreating and in being fruitful and filling the earth.

He did not give this command to two men or to two women. The sovereign God ordained it this way at the very beginning. He even reiterated this when He declared that a man should "leave his father and his mother and shall cleave to his wife, and they shall become one flesh" (Gen. 2:24). It was not two fathers or two mothers; the first marriage was arranged by God, not man. The Divine Creator is the Alpha and the Omega (Rev. 1:8). He is the first Word, and He is the last Word. No man can change that fact. His infinite love created the one man, one woman marriage as a reflection of His holy heart. Anything else is an abomination to Him and goes against His holy mandate. Coming short of that is blatant disobedience that decrees eternal separation from God.

Armageddon is the end-time battle. It defines the final test of this relationship. This global crisis is imminent.

It Began in a Garden

Ladies and gentlemen, we must realize that the first battle began in a garden. The last one will end there, as well. Mankind still asks, "Did God really say…?" (Gen. 3:1). It is the classic compromise of total obedience to God that still wreaks havoc with our souls. In this critical hour, we cannot afford to be disobedient, rebellious children wanting our own apple of fleeting earthly pleasures. It is just too costly! The first question by the first couple on earth is still being asked—but, how shall we answer?

The battle then and now is about our relationship with our Creator. It's about intimacy and true identity. Adam and Eve sinned, thereby relinquishing their close relationship not only with God, but with one another. Life always takes us back to the garden and that same pivotal question, "Did God really say…?" An alert mind and heart will heed the last-days advice of Revelation 2:7: "He who has an ear, let him hear what the Spirit says to the churches. To him who overcomes, I will grant to eat of the tree of life, which is the Paradise of God." Jesus restored intimacy with God, thereby restoring our true identity. Do you know your identity? Together, let's discover it beyond a shadow of a doubt!

We have entered a time of revelation where it is imperative to grasp the full meaning of the most intimate book of the Bible, Song of Songs. Why? Because it describes this holy, intimate relationship we are to have with our Creator. It's a book of intense longing! This Old Testament book is an allegorical love affair of God's Son and His bride, the church. It speaks of that divine intimacy being restored in God's end-time garden dwellers.

The first garden began with only one man and one woman. That's the only marriage that will be allowed back in! Song of Songs 4:11–14 says, "Your lips, my bride, drip honey; honey and milk are under your tongue, and the fragrance of your garments is like the fragrance of Lebanon. A garden locked is my sister, my bride. A rock garden locked, a spring sealed up. Your shoots are an orchard of pomegranates with choice fruits, henna with nard plants, nard and saffron, calamus and cinnamon, with all the trees of frankincense, myrrh and aloes, along with all the finest spices." Some of those same spices were brought to the stable in Bethlehem at the birth of the Son of God. Our Father God again confirmed His covenantal ordination of marriage of one man and one woman by placing Jesus in the home of Mary and Joseph.

Further in that same chapter we find these beautiful words: "You are a garden spring, a well of fresh [living] water, and streams flowing from Lebanon. Awake, O north wind, and come, wind of the south; make my garden breathe out fragrance, let its spices be wafted abroad. May my beloved come into his garden and eat its choice fruits" (Song of Songs 4:15–16). Those gardens are being unlocked and revealed once again. The garden battle for the true Bride of Christ has now emerged into the final stages of the earth's existence.

Take note of this exciting promise given in Isaiah 51:3: "Indeed the Lord will comfort Zion; He will comfort all her waste places. And her wilderness He will make like Eden, and her desert like the garden of the Lord; joy and gladness will be found in her, thanksgiving and sound of a melody." There's great comfort in knowing true love.

One Question

There is only *one question* we are all going to have to answer as this last epic battle commences—*only one.* That question is, "Who am I?" Will we bear the marks of Christ or satan? Have we been branded spiritually on our forehead for obedience or disobedience? For good, or for evil? The stage has been set and decreed from all eternity. It has been recorded so that mankind can know about it and prepare for it. This record is found in the last book of the Bible. Revelation 13:16–18 gives us these startling words, "And he [satan/the beast] causes all, the small and the great, and the rich and the poor, and the free men and the slaves to be given a mark on their right hand, or on their forehead, and he provides that no one should be able to buy or sell, except the one who has the mark, either the name of the beast or the number of his name. Here is wisdom. Let him who has understanding calculate the number of the beast, for the number is that of a *man*; and his number is six hundred and sixty-six."

Mankind will try to manipulate things according to his own pleasures and desires and not that of God. Humans will try to redefine God's covenant to suit their fleshy desires. This is precisely why this beastly mark is that of "man." But God Almighty has His mark as well! Revelation 9:4 declares, "And they were told that they should not hurt the grass of the earth, nor any green thing, nor any tree, but only the men who do *not* have the seal of God on their foreheads."

Who Are You?

So, who are you? Do you or someone you know have an identity crisis? Have you been dealing with uncertainties within your heart? Have there been struggles in the area of intimacy? Have there been struggles in relationships in your life in one form or another? Have there been struggles in areas of sexuality, in fornication, adultery, pornography, homosexuality, lesbianism, prostitution, abortion, or others? Have there been struggles in your life that involve gambling, cussing, gossiping, slander, witchcraft, violence, and other things of the fleshy, lower nature? Is there an uncertainty in your heart as to where you will end up eternally after death? This is your moment in time to ponder your true identity.

There is a fresh urgency rising to delve into what the end-time battle of the ages is *really* going to look like so there won't be any question about who we are and what may happen to us. Let us not be caught unawares. Diabolical sneak attacks by the enemy are happening on a more frequent basis than ever before.

The battle for intimacy with God as Adam and Eve knew it has always been upon us, but now even more so. Do we honestly know the sound of the Lord God walking in the garden in the cool of the day as they did? We can, you know (Gen. 3:8)! However, take note and beware that the world is about to be shaken off its axis! Anything that can be shaken will be shaken (Heb. 12:27).

So what does the Master Maker, the God Almighty, have to say about all these things? We need to know.

PRAYER

Father God of all creation, I desire to know You more! Reveal to me my true identity through Your Son Jesus that I may walk in purity of purpose for all You have for me. Amen.

◆ three ◆

THE ENVY OF THE ENEMY

GOD'S BEST BUSINESS is the reconstruction business! The holy carpenter Jesus came to remodel and restore broken lives and shattered relationships. He came to put His Father's holy designs back into alignment that everyone would know true peace within their hearts. He is the Prince of Peace. If you do not know Him then you need to establish your true identity in Him and peace will come.

Let's continue to consider where this all began. In the Garden of Eden, the first couple had a deep and intimate relationship with God, communing with Him openly, deeply, spirit-to-spirit. They knew the sound of His voice as lovers do. No one says your name like the lover of your soul! The Lord Jesus Himself showed this to us when He tenderly spoke to Mary Magdalene near the garden tomb where His body was laid. He called out her name. But in her distraught condition she was so startled she was not aware it was the Lord. She turned toward Him and recognized the profound power of the sound of His voice and immediately fell at His feet (John 20:16–17). We would do well also to turn toward Him.

Mary's experience in the garden tomb parallels the married couple in the first garden who had known the sound of God's footsteps. They knew that holy sound. They knew it was "Him whom they longed for," because those footsteps were like no other (Ps. 84:2)! This longing aspect is reiterated years later through the Old Testament book Song of Songs as the bride and groom pine for one another.

Adam and Eve knew God's nearness. It was natural for them to hear the sound of their Creator God. They knew His presence as He walked and talked with them through the breathy mist in the cool of the day in this glorious garden—the garden of ecstasy. This was divine communication at its best!

To be able to commune effectively is at the core of every human heart because we all desire the skill to communicate effectively and precisely so we are not misunderstood. Communication is at the heart of the matter. If someone can muddle, fuddle, confuse, and fog up a communiqué, then distortion, half-truths, misunderstandings, and lies begin to spew forth ushering in heartache, pain, disturbance, and disaster. This is what shatters marriages, families, companies, and even whole countries that war against each other.

The First Lady of the Garden knew her covering or headship came from God the Father and secondly from that of her husband, for he was created ahead of her. The young couple had unity of heart as they enjoyed walking the trails of bliss in this magnificent garden of splendor. The young bride was pleased with her soulmate. And the young groom could not be happier with his perfect helpmate. If ever there was wedded bliss, this was it.

Lurking in the Shadows

But trouble was lurking in the shadows. The man and the woman, created in perfection and having divine relationship with Jehovah God, stirred envy in the nether world or dark world of satan and his demonic angels who had preceded them in creation. These angelic beings fell away from God's love by rebelling against Him (Luke 10:8). They could no longer know Him in perfect bliss as did Adam and Eve. This jealousy has raged all through the ages and continues to this day. It will be at the root of the impending greatest battle on earth and will cause an incalculable holocaust at the close of humanity. The unprecedented hate within these fallen angels formed into a dark plan to contaminate and curse this beautiful love affair God had created for this first couple.

These demonic forces saw the love of God bestowed into this fascinating new creation of the man and the woman. They saw the joy of Adam and Eve's close relationship to God and to one another and it was more than satan could bear! He had to find a way to beguile this love affair. Here's where many know how to pick up part of the story for themselves because they know how Eve took the forbidden fruit from satan. They know how she fell from God's favor and presence and how Adam soon joined her in this beguilement, losing all subsequent humanity's intimate relationship with God—until Christ restored it fully on the cross of Calvary. But what many do not know is that this same scenario will be played out to an alarming degree one final time at the conclusion of human existence.

People still have the same choice to make as Adam and Eve. Whose voice will we listen to? Armageddon, the last war of the ages, which is the battle for the Bride of Christ, will be the most intense, horrendous one on the face of the earth. Our enemy satan, along with all his demonic angels, are now unleashing wickedness to intensifying degrees. The enemy of our souls is devising new ways to entice the bride with intrigue and deception to disrupt divine and holy communication from God's Word in Scripture (Ezek. 21:31). Are you aware of these things? How are you going to know the voice of truth of the living God? How are you protecting yourself from the lies and deception of the enemy?

The first bride and groom contaminated themselves with miscommunication. They entertained, pondered, and then fell to satan's webbed words, "Did God really say…?" Maligned truth! Thus the marriage of Adam and Eve then knew sin. After the first bite of the forbidden fruit, their marriage was in big, big trouble. Anything could happen. Mistrust, lies, anger, fear—anything satan wanted to throw at them—was now open game.

The Alarm Clock

The Creator's heart was broken. He had to abandon them in their rebellion. No longer could His glory be displayed in this couple because they had entered into separation, defilement, and deep darkness. They had entered the world of sin, sickness, disease, and death. Lies, deceit, broken covenants, compromise, contamination of truth, and a host of other ungodly things are still resident within those who do not accept God's divine romance through the redemptive plan of Calvary. Indeed the stage is now set for the end of man's final habitation of planet earth. But many either do not know this or are in denial about it.

The alarm clock has been going off day by day. But many turn aside, shut it off, and slumber on. We must wake up. We must rise up! We must be on high alert! Satan is feverishly working his end-time plans in order that he might bring confusion, compromise, and contamination to God's Word for those who either do not know Scripture or for those who mix it with the world's ticklish phraseology. There's a powerful warning in Revelation 22:18–20, "I testify to everyone who hears the words of the prophecy of this book: if anyone adds to them, God shall add to him the plagues which are written in this book; and if anyone takes away from the words of this prophecy, *God shall take away his part from the tree of life* and from the holy city, which are written in this book. He who testifies to these things says, 'Yes, I am coming quickly,' Amen. Come Lord Jesus" (emphasis added). Let us partake only of the fruit of the Holy Spirit! (Gal. 5:22–24).

Probing Question

The probing question by the serpent in the Garden of Eden is still center stage in the battle for the divine relationship God desires to have with every human being. Satan and his cohorts will always entice us with the same words he used against the first couple, "Did God really say…?" (Gen. 3:1). Authority is usurped through his beguilement. It's like a little child who tries to compromise an order given by one of his parents by saying in his mind or heart (or with his mouth!), "Did Daddy really mean what he said that I couldn't play in the street? Why can't I play there? What's he trying to keep me from? What doesn't he want me to see there? I think there's something really neat there and he just doesn't want me to see it or have it! I bet he thinks I'm not mature enough! Well, I'll just show him!" All kinds of self-arguments are engaged when one defies the living God. We've all done it. We've all fallen short of the glory of God and need to be saved from harm and destruction (Rom. 3:23–24).

And so it goes from one generation to the next. Rebellion creeps in like a sly, silent snake into our souls because we want to be in charge of our own lives. We want to be in control and we'll ask the same deadly garden question, "Did God really say....?" And far too often, we want to answer it out of our own selfish desires instead of relying on the wisdom of our Almighty God who made heaven and earth—and us!

In that glorious garden of the Lord at the beginning of time, the divine romance was tested to the breaking point, then shattered. The capsule of time as we know it is about to end and that holy romance is about to be tested one final time. We are nearing the culminating point, the point at which the fight and final destruction is reached. That battle is fiercely raging even as you read this! It is intensifying to a magnitude that's going to astound every living, breathing human being. "Look among the nations! Observe! Be astonished! Wonder! Because I am doing something in your days—You would not believe if you were told" (Hab. 1:5).

What is God doing? What is satan doing? What are you doing?

Prayer

Heavenly Father, I ask You to bring my soul into alertness to hear Your powerful voice over my life. Awaken my soul from its slumbering state that I may know the true pathway to life through Your redemptive plan at Calvary. Show me how to better communicate with You as I seek Your face and Your will for my life. I long to know You up close and personal. Amen.

◆ four ◆

WINNING BACK THE BRIDE

After Adam and Eve turned their backs on the Sovereign God of Truth, it didn't change God's love for them. He *is* love! But as an earthly child disobeys, there are consequences. Some are more severe than others. This couple's disobedience brought the severest of all, complete separation from fellowship with God. Consequently they gave us the inheritance of bad family genes! Our DNA became distorted.

Was this divine relationship lost forever? It appeared to be so. But because God *is* love, He provided a redemptive plan to gain back their intimacy with Him through His Son, Jesus. What a plan! But it's only through the sacrificial Blood of the Lamb of God that we are redeemed. Jesus declared, "I am the way, and the truth, and the life; no one comes to the Father but through Me" (John 14:6). Every human being has the choice to accept or refuse the plan!

When the garden couple fell into sin, changing humanity's history, compromise began to invade all areas of people's lives. Decisions for good or bad had to be made every day. It's the same for us. Many of these daily choices are strategic decisions, affecting our walk with a holy, eternal God, that hold significant consequences. Since Original Sin crept into the picture, people have tested the authority of their Creator beyond their natural, God-ordained limits. Consequently, the unthinkable is now unfolding! Marriage is now in a battle for its very definition! The "death question," "Did God really say…?" is in force more than ever. This beguiling statement continues to break the heart of our Father God!

Perfect Alignment

Those who love God's Word and His Truth will be in perfect alignment with His divinely created "one man, one woman in marriage" covenant. What a divine exclamation point it was when Adam, the first husband on earth, declares his joy upon seeing his bride for the first time, "This is now bone of my bones, and flesh of my flesh; she shall be called, Woman because she was taken out of Man" (Gen. 2:23). As this beautiful woman was taken out of the rib of her husband, it didn't mean she would now think like a man, or have manly features or mannerisms. Nor would Adam have any of the feminine features of his wife. No! God created them to be distinctly different. They were only alike as far as being made into warm flesh and blood with a destiny of eternal fellowship with God (Gen. 2:23).

The Hebrew word for man or husband is *ishi*, and the Hebrew word for woman is *ishshah*. They weren't both called *ishi* nor were they both called *ishshah*, for that would have been an abomination to God. These are not the same names! God made them separate, a male and a female. Man did not come out of man. Woman did not come out of woman. It wasn't that way then, nor can it be now, "For as the woman originates from the man, so also the man has his birth through the woman; and all things originate from God" (1 Cor. 11:12).

Distortion

There was only one man and only one woman in the Garden of Eden. Clearly this is God's statement for the sanctity of marriage. Sanctity, because what God does is always the good thing, the holy thing, the righteous thing. As seen in the just quoted text of Corinthians, this marriage between a man and a woman originated from God Almighty Himself. He established it and sanctified it as a reflection of His holy image. Listen to this! You and I need to know that this is a prophetic forerunner for the marriage of His only begotten Son, who will soon break through the realms of heaven returning to earth a second time to take His bride away! But it won't happen without a big fight! It won't happen without a global, cataclysmic battle for the *true* Bride of Christ! Who is she? We must know beyond a shadow of a doubt!

God the Father told the inhabitants of the earth to "be holy as He is holy" (Exod. 13:13; Lev. 11:44–45). A marriage between one man and one woman is the only holy matrimonial union He established. There is no other. His divine covenants stand forever as decreed all through Scripture. Psalm 89:34–35 declares: "My covenant I will not violate, nor will I alter the utterance of My lips. Once I have sworn by my holiness; I will not lie to David." Not far into the book of Genesis, the Almighty announced in Genesis 9:13, "I set My bow in the cloud, and it shall be for a sign of a covenant between Me and the earth." His divine covenants are not only unchangeable, but eternal.

One can't help but be awed in seeing a glorious rainbow in the skies after a refreshing rain. It's a spectacular confirmation of God's covenant and His holy ordinances written across the very heavens! It's not too surprising then, that satan's beguilement of God's covenant would attempt to distort the beautiful rainbow. The Gay World Pride movement uses it as their own emblem. It's sheer mockery. They can emulate, but they cannot change one letter of God's decrees. The prophet Isaiah bemoans, "So the word of the Lord to them will be, 'order on order, order on order, line on line, line on line, a little here, a little there,' that they may go and stumble backward, be broken, snared and taken captive" (Isa. 28:13). Please understand God loves every one of us! But just as Adam and Eve disobeyed Him, suffering the severest of consequence of separation from God, those who do likewise, dishonoring His covenants, will suffer the same fate unless they repent.

Birthing

As the Garden of Eden experience unfolded for Adam, he named his wife *Eve* because she was the mother of all the living (Gen. 3:20). She could not have been the father of all the living for that doesn't make sense. The first human after Adam and Eve had to be produced by them. Two women cannot produce a baby, nor can two men. It's physically not possible because of God's covenantal designs for procreation of the earth. The Old Testament prophet Jeremiah, who was called the weeping prophet, lamented in chapter 30:5–6 of the book named for him, "For thus says the Lord, 'I have heard a sound of terror, of dread, and there is no peace.

Ask now, and see, if a male can give birth. Why do I see every man with his hands on his loins, as a woman in childbirth? And why have all faces turned pale?" The paleness referred to here has a ghastly meaning in the original Hebrew language: to pervert; to destroy; totally annihilated.[1] This could suggest the devastation of AIDS that comes mostly through homosexuality and other sins of immorality. Unfortunately, this disease is climbing to epic portions in some areas of the world. This could very well be one of the plagues spoken of in the book of Revelation that will occur in the last days (Rev. 16; 22:18).

The phrase "turned pale" is further explained in the *Lexical Aids and Commentaries of the Bible* as a term used in drawing attention to the example of God's just anger on the impenitent cities of Sodom and Gomorrah who were destroyed because of homosexuality and immorality.[2] It is not hard to connect the dots. Let's compute these things. How far has modern society gone in re-enacting the destiny of these two cities? Noteworthy is the fact that the judgment of these condemned communities is recorded so early within the foundational opening book of the Bible. Genesis 19 is just a few chapters away from the ordained couple in the Garden. It wasn't long before perversion against God's laws began to creep in. How could anyone of us ignore these clear and concise messages of an Almighty and fearsome God? Ought we not examine ourselves in light of such an immense Majesty and Power as our Divine Creator and Holy Designer?

It was God's good pleasure to specially design the human body, uniquely fitting male and female together to continue the human race. It was His way of commissioning the First Couple to fulfill His command to "be fruitful and multiply and fill the earth" (Gen. 1:28). This could not have happened had there been two men or two women as the First Couple in the Garden of Eden. This was the first divinely established household. This fist house was one of purity, holiness, and divine purpose.

Astoundingly, one will read headlines in the newspaper announcing the joy of some Hollywood gay or lesbian couple having a child with his or her partner. Of course, the headlines are false. They may have a child in tow, but it still came from the seed of one man and the egg of one woman and conceived in a dish in some laboratory or the child was adopted with great fanfare from some third world nation. There could never be, nor will there ever be, a baby born to two males or two females.

Questionable Birth Certificates

A very interesting concept has begun to emerge these days as more and more countries are sanctioning homosexual marriages presumably due to political pressure. The couples, in these "marriages" are now wanting the birth certificates of their children to read, instead of *mother* and *father,* "Parent A and Parent B." And are we to assume baby makes "C"? This is quite confusing and un-natural.

The global issue of gay marriage is reaching a crescendo as men and women are having a severe identity crisis because of the lies and deceit of the enemy of our souls. Many simply don't have the slightest clue who they are! Why? Because the people of the earth, more than at any other time in our human existence, are questioning all the foundational truths of God's Word. It's not just gay marriage, but the Ten Commandments, life and death issues such as abortion and euthanasia, as well as a host of other things.

Many foundational truths are being shifted to suit one's own desires. This isn't anything new! It's been going on since the Garden of Eden. Something else that hasn't changed is that there's always trouble lurking nearby when one does what he deems is right in his own eyes versus God's. It got Adam and Eve in a heap of trouble affecting every generation! Likewise, our decisions today affect those who come behind us. What legacy are you and I leaving? Is it one of truth or deception?

The Book of Judges in the Bible is aptly named because of the judgments God had to bring time and time again upon His chosen people when they were in direct rebellion to His laws and statutes. Judges 3:4 says that their enemies, "Were for testing Israel to find out if they would obey." Resounding through the centuries are these words: "In those days there was no king in Israel; every man did what was right in his own eyes" (Judg. 17:6). Stated even more profoundly, Proverbs 14:12 says, "There is a way which seems right to a man, but its end is the way of death." Doing things our own, self-centered ways always spells—*trouble*!

God has so designed His own world, His own kingdom, that the laws of nature hold true whether man distorts them or not. What's set is set. The laws of nature stand secure. No one can tame a tornado, no one can calm a hurricane, no one can harness an earthquake. "His works were finished from the foundation of the world" (Heb. 4:3). As in the first garden, satan is still tempting men and women through God's beautiful nature, especially that of the flesh, in order to distort, destroy, rob, and kill. Satan is very bloodthirsty and his goal is complete annihilation!

Not Land, Oil, or Gold

We have now come into a time on the earth where the final epic battle is about to take place. The clock is ticking toward Armageddon. The fight will not be over lands, or oil, or gold as some suppose. It will be over the true Bride of Christ. This isn't the movie *Star Wars*, this one is for real! This one is sure to come. This one will be fought globally as God's matrimonial ceremony and the enemy's distortion of it are fought in every nation! We must set ourselves on high alert and prepare for this emerging Armageddon battle of the ages that's looming ever nearer. This war will be like none other. More people will die than at any other time in history. But the fear factor will not be played for those who are the true Bride of Christ! "Perfect love casts out fear, because fear involves punishment, and the one who fears is not perfected in love" (1 John 4:18). So rejoice, this is good news!

The bride is defined as the whole of God's people, the redeemed of the Lord, those saved, those who have accepted Christ's work on the Cross of Calvary. Scripture clearly states this in many places and in various ways. Revelation 21:9 is especially precise, "Come here, I shall show you the bride, the wife of the Lamb." Who is the Lamb? Who is the Bridegroom? It is none other than Jesus who came to take away the sins of the world. He Himself has likened His relationship to His Church as a Bride, a virgin, a lover, an intimate relationship of spirit to spirit without spot or wrinkle (Eph. 5:27).

The Word of God declares that "Deep calls to deep" (Ps. 42:7). God so designed mankind that the innermost part of us cries out for intimacy so that our deepest needs be met. It can only come by way of knowing from whence we came in the first place. God creates every human being after His own image. Therefore that image is holy and ordained by Him. An *ishi,* or man, is created to be just that, a man. An *ishshah,* or woman, is created to be just that, a woman. Every heart, by virtue of the design of God, has a desire to fellowship with God, talk with Him, and know Him personally. It is the cry in every soul whether recognized or not. It's ingrained. Man's blood, his heart, his very being, cries out for intimacy and that's the great love affair! It's between the soul of man and his Creator, his Maker, his Designer.

In the opening chapters of humanity, God bestows upon the first two human beings an earthly companion, complimenting one another in which to walk through life. That companion is the only rightful one ordained for them. It's the only *holy* companionship He created for marriage. Anything else is an abomination.

Physical and Spiritual Intimacy

The cry for intimacy is loud and clear! Consider the amazing fact how God created within the human race a fulfillment for both body *and* soul. He has set a divine covenant in order for intimacy in both the natural realm and in the spiritual realm. Therefore, flesh that is surrendered to God is in alignment with Him. A soul that is surrendered to Him is in alignment as well. His unique designs of co-joined flesh of a man and a woman in marriage wonderfully fulfill His divine will on earth. John 3:6 is clear on this: "That which is born of the flesh is flesh, and that which is born of the Spirit is spirit." It's time we look to God and His ways for they are certainly higher than ours! Who are we to argue with one so high, divine, holy, majestic, and powerful? Who are we to redefine marriage? Job 40:1 aptly says, "Then the Lord said to Job, 'Will the faultfinder contend with the Almighty? Let him who reproves God answer it.'" (See also Isaiah 55:8–9.)

You and I need to examine ourselves in light of this. What's in our hearts? What do we want? Are we in love with our Creator, Maker, Designer, and Savior, wanting to please Him above all else? Or are we looking for love in all the wrong places?

Do you desire companionship and intimacy that transcends time and space that goes beyond anything of this world? Do you long for a love so deep and so satisfying it defies human definition? Wouldn't it be wonderful to know a fulfillment in your heart and soul that satisfies deeper than you could ever imagine?

It is possible. Let shouts of joy pour forth from your lips! People, it is not only possible, but an absolute reality! God the Father has made a way for us to know Him in a way that defies human, fleshy definition or experience. His divine Word tells us spiritual things are spiritually discerned. Flesh gives birth to flesh in human marriages, but spirit gives birth to spirit in the spiritual, heavenly marriage. Psalm 16:11 is a breathtaking statement, "Thou wilt make known to me the path of life; in Thy Presence is fullness of joy; in Thy right hand there are pleasures forever." His pleasures are glorious!

Prayer

Dear Lord God, I come to You asking for revelation of truth and knowledge. Keep me from the deceiver! Help me to walk in godly, holy love as ordained by You from the foundation of the world. Make known to me the paths of life that I may know Thy pleasures forevermore. Amen.

◆ five ◆

COMPROMISE— A LUKEWARM DISH

REMODELING PROJECTS ARE messy. Sometimes you'll have things scattered everywhere. Oh, the clutter of it all. But the end result is so wonderful. Did you know God loves remodeling projects? He's very fond of taking a broken, shattered life and reconstructing it according to His purposes that it might reflect His glory! God has His best designs on you. Hallelujah.

Now if you have ever done a remodeling project, perhaps adding a bedroom or family room, you are well aware that a good solid foundation has to be laid. Otherwise, the whole project would disintegrate. Eternal truth declares to us in Psalm 127:1 that unless the Lord builds the house, its builders labor in vain. Therefore, it is in our best interest that we not sway from the true family paradigm God has set in place. His pure and holy love is the criteria for building a beautiful home. An imitation or false kind of love will bring it to ruin. We must be like Abraham who was looking for a place with "foundations whose architect and builder is God" (Heb. 11:10).

Adam and Eve were the founding couple, the bedrock if you will, for all subsequent mankind. The marriage between a man and a woman is divinely set up. It's set in stone, the Rock of Ages:

> Therefore everyone who hears these words of Mine and acts upon them, may be compared to a wise man, who built his house upon a rock. [The paradigm or foundation, which is Jesus Christ.] And the rain descended and the floods came, and the winds blew, and burst against that house; and yet it did not fall, for it had been founded upon the rock. And everyone who hears these words of Mine and does not act upon them, will be like a foolish man, who built his house upon the sand. And the rains descended, and the floods came, and the winds blew, and burst against that house; and it fell, and great was its fall.
>
> —Matthew 7:24–27

Crisis

Our homes are in crisis! Foundations are cracking. Families are under severe attack. Divorces are at record levels. There are more runaway, kidnapped, and abused children. This is not only happening out in the world, but sadly in the house of God as well, "'Even in My house I have found their wickedness,' declares the Lord" (Jer. 23.11). Jeremiah 23:14 compares these "goings on" of today to the days of Sodom and Gomorrah, which God destroyed because of their wickedness in many things, especially sexual perversion. Many churches have crumbled because of fallen leaders who have been deceived and lured into political correctness. The world's way has been, and always will be, to seek the favor of men rather than God. We need to examine ourselves with the question, "Do I look to men or God for affirmation and fulfillment?"

Compromise on many fronts has caused a huge crack in the foundation that God set in place. Unheard of in generations past, churches are ordaining homosexuals and lesbians. (I will speak more about this topic in another chapter.) Too many priests, pastors, deacons, and church leaders are abusing men, women, and children in unprecedented numbers. Rampant deceit and compromise are fast becoming a plague in far too many houses of God. It is beginning to rival the Dark Ages! Again looking to the truth found in the Bible, Jeremiah says in 23:36, "For you will no longer remember the oracle of the Lord, because every man's own word will become the oracle, and you have perverted the words of the living God, the Lord of hosts, our God." In case you have been living on another planet, human beings can be very stubborn and selfish. We want our own way. Only a heart yielded to God can find victory over these things.

Favor of Men or God?

Our eternal bedrock is a holy, fearful, powerful, Almighty God. In the Bible we read of a priest named Eli, who defied divine orders by allowing impure things to go on right under his nose. Oh, the audacity of a human soul that assumes its behavior is hidden! He who made the eyes does He not see all things? (See Psalm 94:9.) It would behoove us therefore to live in complete awareness of this fact.

In 1 Samuel 2 the priest Eli was having a struggle disciplining his rebellious sons who were leaders in temple church. He was supposed to keep them accountable. But something happened. Things got a bit slothful, selfish, and sinful. "Whatever feels good, do it," seemed to be the order of the day. Unfortunately the highest authority in the land and above the land into the eternal realm declares to us, "A way may seem right to a man, but in the end it leads to death" (Prov. 14:2).

Compromise ran rampant in the temple. Eli at one point does make a feeble attempt to correct his boys. But God says the righteous are as bold as a lion and he failed to be bold and firm enough to hold them accountable (Prov. 28:1). We don't have to be in people's faces, but we certainly have to keep the faith.

Maybe Eli didn't want to make waves or upset the apple cart. Maybe he compromised on too many things in order to keep peace in the house. Maybe he was trying to be politically correct rather than being godly correct. Maybe his career kept him busy with other things. Who knows? But verse 29 does tell us how Eli was himself gorged with the fat of the offerings and apparently wanted the favor of men (his sons) more than that of God. That can't be good. The apostle Paul warns of this sort of thing centuries later when he writes, "For am I now seeking the favor of men, or of God?" (Gal. 1:10).

Is this what the church has done? Are we more desirous of pleasing the world so we can look, smell, and act like everyone else? That philosophy certainly keeps us in a much more comfortable zone, but immediately takes us out of God's zone of righteousness. Where do *you* want to be?

Set Apart

Jehovah God explicitly commands in Deuteronomy 14:2 that His desire is for a "peculiar" people, set apart from all the rest. Standing on His holy foundation, going against the grain of worldly opinion or being politically incorrect will no doubt make us oddly peculiar. We are supposed to stand out in a crowd! "I did not sit in the circle of merrymakers, nor did I exult, because of Thy hand upon me, I sat alone, for Thou didst fill me with indignation" (Jer. 15:17). Eli didn't have much indignation within his soul when he saw the unholy things going on around Him. He did not have the inner discipline or integrity to exclude his own self from these "temple charades." Let us resolve that there will be no fear of man whatsoever in our bones! If God is for us, who can be against us? (Rom. 8:31).

Unfortunately, we're seeing the evil of compromise creep in unawares. It's a sly snake just as it was in the first garden. The confrontational question, "Did God really say that?" has continued.

Picking up the story again about Eli in 1 Samuel 2, verse 22 says, "Now Eli was very old; and he heard all that his sons were doing to all Israel and how they lay with the women who served at the doorway of the tent of meeting. And he said to them, 'Why do you do such things, the evil things that I hear from the people? No, my sons; for the report is not good which I heard the Lord's people circulating.'" Later in that chapter it goes on to say how the boys would not listen to the voice of their father. This was open, blatant rebellion of the first degree! Sounds like some of us as well. I can relate in saying, "Been there, done that!" Personally, I needed Father God! We all do. He loves us very deeply and desires that we be holy inhabitants in His house. He's standing at the door knocking. Let's open up! (Rev. 3:19–22).

Eli's boys were beyond just being prodigal sons because the prodigal in Luke 15 at least finally came to his senses and returned to his father. The Lord is actively looking for prodigals. Are you one of them? If so, come home. God the Father is waiting with open arms of love for those who will come clean and repent: "I urge you therefore, brethren, by the mercies of God, to present your bodies a living and holy sacrifice, acceptable to God, which is your spiritual service of worship" (Rom. 12:1). We are called to worship the Lord in spirit and in truth with our entire being (John 4:24). We can do this! Surrendering to God and His plans and purposes for our lives is the key.

Faithful

God's heart in this passage of Samuel was crying out for a true priest who would do the holy thing and hold the line of righteousness and holiness in his home and in the temple: "But I will raise up for Myself a faithful priest who will do according to what is in My heart and in My soul; and I will build him an enduring house, and he will walk before My anointed always" (1 Sam. 2:35).

Wait a minute! What was that? An enduring house? Yes. And who was that faithful priest God raised up? It was Samuel, a man who kept the lamp of God burning even in the presence of Eli and his rebellious sons. Have we done that? Have we kept the lamp of God burning deep within us even if we're surrounded by rebellion and unbelief?

Samuel kept his eyes on the burning lamps in the temple and knew within his spirit the passage in Revelation 3:16 before it was ever written, "So because you are lukewarm, and neither hot nor cold, I will spit you out of My mouth." He saw the jeopardy of compromise and purposed in his own heart not to become lukewarm, or worse yet, cold! He stayed hot for God! Are we?

This holy prophet, Samuel, actually did what he was supposed to do in the house of God. He ministered to the Lord first, then to the people. He stayed true to the priorities of God, keeping the first commandment first. Imagine that! This isn't supposed to be unique, but sadly, much of the church world today has almost forgotten that. More often than not, it's all about a nice Sunday morning service in a nice sanctuary, with nice surroundings, nice air-conditioning, a few nice songs, comfy pews, fleshy-dressy clothes, and a fast-food Word of God sermon so people can be out the door within an hour. No upsets. No disruptions. No deliverances. No salvations. No healings. No homeruns on the playing field of the church's own agenda. Lord, have mercy!

Clean House

It's time to clean house! Some people falsely think they are OK and haven't a clue to the fact they are living on the precipice of an eternal hell by not obeying Father God. Anyone who has known a "hell on earth" situation cannot begin to imagine the hell satan has open to us!

God has ordained us to be His living temples (2 Cor. 6:16). So, beware of Leviticus 14 that speaks of the house, which has been plagued with a malignant mark and needs to be cleansed. What's in your house? Or your heart? Whose house are you living in? Who are you, and "whose" are you? Are you a godly bride or a worldly bride? Are you living in a house of cards, gambling away purity and holiness? Are there cracks in your foundation? Have you detected some broken mortar and crumbling walls? Have you compromised the Word of God and His truth?

Some are already in critical condition according to Revelation 3:16's description of a wishy-washy, compromising, lukewarm heart. For them, there may not be enough time to make a desperate 9-1-1 call to God at the moment of entering eternity. The volcanic battle of all time is soon to be upon us. There is no time to lose in checking the condition of your soul. As with Eli and his sons, compromise is a damning thing. Take note. Take charge. Take God's way.

Prayer

Precious Lord, guard my heart that I may not compromise any portion of Your Word. Teach me to be a faithful servant in Your house. I want to serve You wholeheartedly all the days of my life. Amen.

◆ six ◆

IDENTITY CRISIS

THERE'S POWER IN the blood—wonder-working power!

Checking the pulse of the heartbeat of the church, we see low blood pressure. Low is not good! A medical digest on the Internet describes low blood pressure as "pressure that is so low it causes symptoms or signs due to the low flow of blood through the arteries and veins. When the flow of blood is too low to deliver enough oxygen and nutrients to vital organs such as the brain, heart, and kidney, the organs do not function normally and may be permanently damaged."[1] It goes on to state that people with prolonged low blood pressure are quite often dehydrated which eventually will lead to further complications if one does not drink enough water. Get the picture?

Some in the house of God have been experiencing low blood pressure spiritually. There just isn't enough of the saving blood of Jesus flowing through their hearts. Yes, it may be pumping in, but it quickly pumps back out due to a lack of living water!

Compromised lifestyles and sinful ways cause blockages. Thus there is an obstruction of the pure flow of power the Lamb of God wants to release over surrendered hearts. Consequently, they're drying up, dying on the vine, becoming dehydrated, and placing themselves in great danger. It is time to call on Dr. Jesus (John 4:7–24).

An Arrested Heart

Do not allow low blood pressure to seep into your spiritual life. It causes lukewarmness and lethargy. Lethargy can be lethal! (Rev. 3:16). God is looking for red-blooded believers. He is trying to raise our awareness of the power of the blood of Calvary so we can have a surging heart rate in our spirit being! He wants us arrested by the Holy Spirit! He really does want us to lose our lives in total abandon to His will and to His ways. So let us happily grasp Galatians 2:20, "I have been crucified with Christ; and it is no longer I who live, but Christ lives in me; and the life which I now live in the flesh I live by faith in the Son of God, who loved me, and delivered Himself up for me."

According to these living words, if we've had a true heart change by encountering the Lamb of God, then we know who we are. We're dead men walking! This is good! Our fleshy desires are dead to sin. Romans 6:11 states it this way, "Even so consider yourselves to be dead to sin, but alive to God in Christ Jesus." Temptations of the flesh will always try to creep in on a daily basis, and that's why Paul exhorts us to die daily to our selfish nature (1 Cor. 15:21). We must learn to get up in the morning and make a new heart-driven commitment of surrendering ourselves to the ways of God and not our own.

Having the wonderful knowledge of who we are in Christ empowers us to "deny ungodliness and worldly desires and to live sensibly, righteously and godly in the present age," no matter what this present age tells us (Titus 2:12). Society hasn't changed much since Eli's day in 1 Samuel. Many people are still seekers of fleshy pleasures and would rather go with the wind of worldly opinion than with the wind of the Holy Spirit. How long shall we vacillate between two opinions? (See 1 Kings 18:21.) Are we on God's side or that of perishable man? The war is definitely on—whose side are you on?

Who Do You Think You Are?

Heaven and hell are asking people the same question: "Who do you think you are?" Satan wants that question mocked in the light of God's truth. The enemy of your soul really wants you to question that because if you don't know the answer, he can fill your mind with doubt, fear, pride, arrogance, and turmoil.

God the Father wants you to know exactly who you are as His child in the light of His truth. He wants us full of faith, savoring all the inheritance of righteousness that's ours through His Son who paid the price for our redemption through His shed blood. Certainly we have all sinned and need to be cleansed, washed, and set free. We have all messed up at some point in our lives because we live in fallen flesh. There isn't a human being who's not fallen short of the glory of God. So why not just fess up and start new and fresh? There's tremendous joy that floods your heart when you come under the canopy of God's covenant of truth and holiness in Christ Jesus (Rom. 3:23). Being bathed is so refreshing! (John 5:1–9).

Understand this—our holy Designer, God Almighty, fabricated each one of us to be used as a vessel of honor for His glory. Unfortunately there will be loss of eternal life for those who allow their lower nature to be used in a dishonoring way, whether it's lying, cheating, stealing, cussing, gossiping, committing fornication, adultery, homosexuality, or anything that's ungodly. A pertinent scripture about house cleaning our living vessels is found in 2 Timothy 2:19–22, "Nevertheless, the firm foundation of God stands, having this seal. 'The Lord knows those who are His,' and 'Let everyone who names the name of the Lord abstain from wickedness.' Now in a large house there are not only gold and silver vessels, but also vessels of wood and of earthenware, and some to honor and some to dishonor. Therefore, if a man cleanses himself from these things, he will be a vessel for honor, sanctified useful to the Master, prepared for every good work. Now flee from youthful lusts, and pursue righteousness, faith, love and peace, with those who call on the Lord from a pure heart." (See also Romans 9:6–33.) We need clean containers!

Prayer Patrol

The past five years, our own ministry of Intimacy With God, has had an inner city Prayer Patrol where we walk the streets asking people a simple question, "Do you need prayer for anything?" It's a simple gesture of getting people to open up and share their heart. It's easy evangelism. Quite often, tears may begin to well up in their eyes as they are touched by the fact that someone cares.

One day we encountered someone sitting in a van parked along the street. We approached asking the usual question if they needed prayer for anything. We got a rather surprising answer. The person behind the wheel said, "Do you want to pray for the man in me, or the woman in me?" Somewhat taken aback, I responded by the power of the Holy Spirit, "Well, God knows who you are. Can we still pray with you?" He said yes. When we were done praying, he invited us to his church where he said all kinds of sexual preferences are welcome and everyone can be who they want to be. We said, "No, thank you," and went on our way. But the holy name of Jesus was declared over this one, and our prayer is that he relives that encounter over and over again in his heart because God loves him and is after him!

I believe this event was a divine intersection of time that the pure gospel of Jesus would be presented to this man. Seeds of grace were planted (Luke 8:4–15). He will have to make a choice for eternal life or death. The Lord presents this option in Deuteronomy 30:19, "I call heaven and earth to witness against you today, that I have set before you life and death, the blessing and the curse. So choose life in order that you may live, you and your descendants, by loving the Lord your God, by obeying His voice, and by holding fast to him; for this is your life and the length of your days." Let us choose wisely. The Word again declares in the same book, "A woman shall not wear man's clothing, nor shall a man put on a woman's clothing; for whoever does these things is an abomination to the Lord your God" (Deut. 22:5). The Lord doesn't mince His Words! Again he declares through Paul in 1 Corinthians 6:9, "Or do you not know the unrighteous shall not inherit the kingdom of God? Do not be deceived; neither fornicators, nor idolaters, nor adulterers, nor effeminate, nor homosexuals, nor thieves, nor the covetous, nor drunkards, nor revilers, nor swindlers shall inherit the kingdom of God."

To Seek and Save

Indeed the scriptures declare that Jesus came to seek and save that which was lost (Luke 19:10). Our encounter that day with this dear man had been no happenstance meeting. We didn't condemn him of his waywardness (he already knew). The Holy Spirit's best business is conviction, not condemnation. However, we must realize there are eternal consequences for all our decisions. We didn't hand him a tract or a Bible. (We have given those out as well.) But, whereas some may toss the tract, or lay aside the Word of God, what we did give him was an encounter of *love*—the love of Jesus! People never forget love!

If you are a believer, what drew you to Christ? Was it condemnation or love? Love can bring one's heart into convicting tears of repentance. And we see this quite often on the streets of our city on Prayer Patrol. Certainly this particular fellow was lost and confused as to who he was. Unfortunately, his church had only added to that confusion with compromise, contamination, deception, and corruption. He wasn't the only one who had an identity crisis; his church did as well.

People need to know who they are. It's a basic human need. Every man and woman was created to be a child of God, but they must choose whether they want to be or not. They must choose if they want life in the family of God or death, which is life outside God's holy covenants. God does not make mistakes when He creates a man or a woman. It's people who make mistakes! Coming to the Lord assures your unmistaken identity. Anything less is confusion.

Conformed to His Death

Jesus states in Matthew 19:4, "Have you not read, that He who created them from the beginning made them male and female." God didn't mince or mix His Words. He said what He meant and meant what He said. He didn't do a half-and-half make up of a person, leaving them to wonder which gender they really are. God is not the author of confusion. Satan is. And God cannot fellowship with confusion (1 Cor. 14:33; Ezra 9:7). If God made you a man, then that's what you are. If God made you a woman, that's what you are. Can it be changed? Is it reversible? Of course. People have surgeries to make it so. But listen now—*this act is the result of an ungodly power arising from the lower nature of the flesh that has not died to Christ and been conformed to His death.* In gender confusion therefore, the flesh is very much alive with all its lusts and desires. Self-gratification reigns rather than living unto a holy God of righteousness. The Almighty decries humanity's confusion in Jeremiah 7:19 when He says, "'Do they spite Me?' declares the Lord. 'Is it not themselves they spite, to their own shame?'" The Lord is looking for purity in all of us!

The book you are now reading is not going to probe into so-called scientific evidence for homosexuality or any other behavior in opposition to God's natural laws and His holy Scripture. Its purpose is to spur you on to seek His truth in His written Word, the Bible, to find out for yourself what is right and wrong. Because when it all shakes down at the very end of life, it will be *the final Word.*

As professing Christians, if we do not know God's Word, then our world can very easily and quickly become neutralized and discolored. Always—*always*—seek out the scriptures to be balanced in your theology. Do not be found wanting, having tipped the scales in an unholy manner (Dan. 5:27).

See for Yourself

We need to caution ourselves from this passage in Romans 1:18–28 and 32, but I encourage you to read it in its entirety that you may see these things for yourself:

> "For the wrath of God is revealed from heaven against all ungodliness and unrighteousness of men, who suppress the truth in unrighteousness, because that which is known about God is evident within them; for God made it evident to them. For since the *creation* of the world His invisible attributes, His eternal power and divine nature, have been clearly seen, being understood through what has been made, so that they are *without excuse*. For even though they knew God, they did not honor Him as God, or give thanks; but they became futile in their speculations, and their *foolish heart* was darkened. Professing to be wise, they became fools, and exchanged the glory of the incorruptible God for an image in the form of corruptible man and of birds and four-footed animals and crawling creatures. Therefore God gave them over in the lusts of their hearts to impurity, that their bodies might be dishonored among them. For they exchanged the *truth* of God for a *lie*, and worshipped and served the creature rather than the Creator, who is blessed

> forever. Amen. For this reason God gave them over to degrading passions; for their women exchanged the natural function for that which is unnatural, and in the same way also the men abandoned the natural function of the woman and burned in their desire toward one another, men with men committing indecent acts and receiving in their own persons the due penalty of their error. And just as they did not see fit to acknowledge God any longer, God gave them over to a depraved mind, to do those things which are not proper...and although they *know* the ordinance of God, that those who practice such things are worthy of death, they not only do the same, but also give hearty approval to those who practice them."

Revelation!

It shouldn't be a shock to anyone that we've all indulged the flesh in one form or another, to one degree or another, since we've all sinned and fallen short of the glory of God (Rom 3:23). But it's a wonderful comfort to know our lives can be cleaned up by the work of Christ's blood at Calvary. Washed, cleansed, and made whole, we become a *new creation* in Christ (2 Cor. 5:17). We come alive in the Spirit and old things pass away along with all the baggage of the flesh. All sorrow, heartache, pain, fear, bitterness, unforgiveness—any and all harassments of the enemy from our yesterdays can be deleted in a moment with the Lamb's stripes, which He endured for this very reason. One moment of prayer accepting this marvelous gift from our Savior Jesus and one is born again into a new life of wholeness and purity.

We are on our way to becoming a pure, holy Bride of Christ without spot or wrinkle! (Eph. 5:27). The bride, the body of Christ worldwide, must be walking in the truth of the Holy Spirit. And that my friend is how you come to know who you are—through the love and grace of Jesus Christ (John 1:17). There's only one way to know who you are and that is through the revelation of the Lamb of God who was slaughtered for sinful flesh.

The world will try to sell us a bill of goods and tell us otherwise. It will try to distort, twist, and contaminate His truth. But why wouldn't it? It's the world! It's not surprising is it? Let us be spiritually educated. After all, there is absolutely no comparison whatsoever to an Almighty, everlasting God to that of which His own breath created! We are the work of His hands. We have a glorious destiny in Him. The Spirit of grace and truth declares, "No one can come to Me, unless the Father who sent Me draws him; and I will raise him up on the last day" (John 1:16; 6:44). So come as you are and let the cross change your life!

Toward the end of the story of mankind when Armageddon will come knocking on our door, we will be comforted by Revelation 7:14, knowing those in the body of Christ are washed and made clean in the blood of the Lamb. Do you want to be washed white as snow (Isa. 1:18)? Do you want a new lease on life? Do you know fellowship and intimacy with your Creator? If not, why not? What road have you been walking? Has it been the highway of holiness in God's ordained ways? Or has it been the bumpy road of doubt, fear, confusion, and self-focus? Do you know that God's thoughts and ways are higher than yours (Isa. 35:8; 55:6–9)?

Have you had an arresting in your heart by the Lord Jesus with death to your flesh?

If not, isn't it time? Do it right now! He loves you!

Prayer

Dear Lord Jesus, I come to You with a heart full of questions, but I know Your Word will answer all of them. I know I have sinned against You. Please forgive me and help me turn my life around with complete surrender to You. I thank You for Your sacrifice for me on the cross. Thank You for saving me and making me a new creation in You. I praise Your wonderful name! Amen.

◆ seven ◆

PERSECUTION

THERE IS AN intense desire for *us* in the Lord's heart. He loves us so much He can hardly wait to wrap His arms around us forever and ever. What an astounding love He has for His people!

Jesus said when He left the earth that He would come again to take His bride, the church, to be with Him forever in heaven. He's looking for heart-to-heart contact, intimacy if you will, desiring a close personal relationship with everyone who is under His Bridegroom covering (Ruth 3:9). He—may I say it again—*He* is coming for His bride. Revelation 19:7–8 beautifully says, "Let us rejoice and be glad and give the glory to Him, for the marriage of the Lamb has come and His bride has made herself ready. And it was given to her to clothe herself in fine linen, bright and clean; for the fine linen is the righteous acts of the saints."

Contrarily, Revelation 18:23 reveals a different kind of wedding that is unholy and condemning. It speaks of Babylon, which represents the world with its philosophies. Of course, it always runs contrary to God's Word, "And the light of lamp will not shine in you any longer; and the voice of the bridegroom and bride will not be heard in you any longer; for your merchants were the great men of the earth, because all the nations were deceived by your sorcery. And in her was found the blood of prophets and of saints, and of all who have been slain on the earth."

Since abominations are apparent in this passage of Scripture, the bridegroom and bride mentioned here might very well be unholy marital unions the world is now sanctioning. Beware! The merchants of the world, the ungodly politicians, the corrupted corners of the church world, are now promoting and sanctioning unholy matrimonial unions at great risk to their souls. Sadly, the blood in this passage refers to the blood of prophets and servants of God who tried to speak forth God's unchangeable Word at the risk of their lives. The bloody battle for the true bride is raging! But it's going to be her finest hour! Hallelujah!

Babylon

The Babylon system of the world is not only increasing but also gaining momentum. Those who sanction gay marriages are being deceived. But they are also the ones who stand to gain significantly in the worldly, political, economic arena because it will help them advance in the marketplace. Political correctness doesn't line up with God's laws! And a darker fate may be on the horizon for Christians who refuse to bow to the pressures of ungodly governments who will enact laws for employment benefits for gay/lesbian couples. (It's happening already!) And because these precious saints cannot or will not in good conscience be able to sanction unholy unions by giving insurance benefits, they will be in jeopardy of losing their own jobs, businesses, homes—everything.

These believers will also be ostracized and persecuted for not agreeing with the majority of the land.

This persecution will be precipitated by many government authorities issuing decrees, as they did regarding our Jewish friends, that no one is to engage in buying or selling with those who do not comply with their standards or they'll suffer the consequences. Everyone in town will know who they are because a mark or a microchip will identify them, as computers now do! It will bear a ghastly resemblance to the Jewish communities in 1930s Germany who had to wear armbands as a distinguishing mark. This mark eventually led them to the death camps! (Matt. 24:9).

PRECARIOUS DAYS

These are precarious days we are now living in. Great persecution will begin to break out globally against uncompromising Christians, who have passionate love for our holy, powerful, and majestic Lord of lords and King of kings. Something far worse than the magnitude of the Holocaust of World War II will begin to unfold. Does this sound absurd to you? Think again. The *unthinkable* happened to the Jewish people. Do not be naïve. There is indeed an end-time battle of the ages coming. Almighty God has said so! It is decreed in His Word and it's very clear this battle will be for the Bride of Christ. It's a battle about holy and unholy intimacy. The book of Revelation reads, "And the dragon was enraged with the woman, and went off to make war with the rest of her offspring, who keep the commandments of God and hold to the testimony of Jesus" (Rev. 12:7).

As this fierce and deadly battle begins to unfold, there will be no fear in God's people. Quite the contrary! Remember, perfect love casts out fear (1 John 4:18). And wonderfully, God assures us those will be spectacular days of His glory appearing brighter and brighter (Isa. 60). It will transcend anything His people have ever known since the foundation of the earth. They will be radiant with His light. It will be an overcoming, overwhelming heavenly light similar to that of Stephen, who even while being stoned to death, had the brilliance of God's glory resting on his face. It shone like that of an angel! (See Acts 6:15; 7:55–56.) That same heavenly light was upon Moses, who when others beheld this powerful, godly glow, became afraid (Exod. 34:30). People will begin to fear the living God in you and me, just as they did with Moses. Why? Because God's truth is light and light exposes hidden, dark lies, deceit, and sin. It will expose them for who they really are!

But understand this, just as in some parts of the world where severe and deadly persecution exists, some will die. Others will be spared (Heb. 11). Either way, the world is going to see God's glory displayed with the holy, reverential fear of God falling everywhere. "But where sin increased, grace abounded all the more" (Rom. 5:20). Accountability for who we are will take place! It will be a worldwide identity crisis. The courts of heaven will be in session passing down divine judgments. It will be Isaiah 60:2 lived out to a great and tremendous degree, "For behold, darkness will cover the earth, and deep darkness the peoples; but the Lord will rise upon you, and His glory will appear upon you."

Maybe you don't want the glory. Do you want it? How much do you want it? We need to discover how hungry we really are for the manifestation of God's glory. This is a new hour, a new time, as a new epic move of God's

Spirit invades the earth. We need revelation, knowledge, insight, understanding, and the reverential fear of God more than at any other time in human history!

The Natural Precedes the Spiritual

Many of the political systems of the world are contaminated. An unprecedented number of judges in the world's court systems are wearing robes of unrighteousness sanctioning gay marriages that are and will be under God's wrathful judgment. People are calling right things wrong, and wrong things right. God told us this would happen! "Woe to those who call evil good, and good evil; who substitute darkness for light and light for darkness; who substitute bitter for sweet and sweet for bitter!" (Isa. 5:20). Barely can anyone blush any more! This doesn't surprise the Lord, either. He said that would happen as well. "Everyone deals falsely. And they have healed the brokenness of My people *superficially*, saying, 'Peace, peace,' but there is no peace. Were they ashamed because of the abomination they have done? They were not even ashamed at all; they did not even know how to blush" (Jer. 6:13–15).

Can Christianity continue to declare peace to those who are lost in their sins? We've been sold a bill of goods by the enemy who keeps pounding us with the same compromising question, "Did God really say…?" Lukewarm Christians are quite often the ones who haven't read Scripture in its entirety, or not at all. We must begin to seek the Lord Jesus in truth through His Word and by the power of the Holy Spirit. Otherwise we will live a lifestyle that pleases our lower nature.

Just as Jesus' first coming was contended for, so it will be again. No sooner had His feet lifted off the earth after His Resurrection, than the fight was on for His bride! Do you feel this struggle? Are you even aware of it? Are you aware of the end-time Armageddon that will wipe away a third of mankind (Rev. 9:15, 18, 20–21)?

It's no surprise that a bridal battle is spreading all over the map. The natural precedes the spiritual according to 1 Corinthians 10:46. The test for the true bride is happening physically, as a precursor for the spiritual. Nation upon nation is now redefining God's ordained covenant of marriage with the ungodly seal of gay/lesbian marriages. But God's uniquely designed relationship of the one man, one woman marriage established in the Garden of Eden was even realized in the animal kingdom when He told Noah to bring a male and female into the Ark that they might be saved from the floods. The reason of course was so they could reproduce and fill the earth once God's judgment had subsided. We see this plainly in Genesis 7:2–3 and 9 where God says, "You shall take with you every clean animal by sevens, a male and his female; and of the animals that are not clean two, a male and his female; also of the birds of the sky, by sevens, male and female, to keep offspring alive on the face of all the earth."

The Burnt Offering

Some may think that the offset number of seven in this passage, which didn't complete a pair, may have made room for homosexuality. But that of course is not true. God required the odd number, so that one of them might be used for a burnt offering to the Lord, leaving the remaining three pairs of males and females to fulfill the Word of the Lord, "Then Noah built an altar to the Lord, and took of every clean animal and of every clean bird and offered burnt offerings on the altar" (Gen. 8:20).

Our burnt offering is our flesh. This command still stands. We enter into that offering through the bloody sacrifice of Jesus' death on the cross. Seven is also God's number of completion and perfection. What is set by God cannot be changed by man, though he may try. Out of the sacrificial Lamb's mouth He declares in Matthew 19:4–6:

> 'Haven't you read,' he replied, 'that at the beginning the Creator made them male and female, and said, 'For this reason a man will leave his father and mother and be united to his wife, and the two will become one flesh? So they are no longer two, but one. Therefore what God has joined together, let man not separate.'

As it was in the beginning, so it shall be at the end. Those who shall be saved will be those who will march to God in a holy manner under the shadow of the cross. Holiness and purity are still demanded by our Creator. The end of the story as recorded in Revelation's last chapter in verse 15 tells us clearly that immoral persons will be left out of God's Presence and will not be able to gain entry into heaven. So it's not just about homosexuality, it's about every immoral act under the sun whether it's pornography, living together without being married, adultery, rape, murder, slander, revenge, anger, or a host of other sins that cut away at pure, godly living. We all need Jesus!

EXPOSED NAKEDNESS

There is a pertinent part of the Bible in Genesis 9:20–25 that we need to address here. Noah, having left the Ark and rebuilding his life, let down his guard. It's somewhat similar to Eli's story and his sons in 1 Samuel. Noah grew lukewarm in his service to God. One day he became inebriated from the fruit of his vineyard and "uncovered himself." As the effect of the wine wore off, he discovered that his son had seen him naked and cursed him!

Looking at a number of commentaries, the question is asked, "Did some unspeakable thing happen that he cursed his own son?" We don't know, but whatever took place must have been despicable and very sinful in order for Noah to do such a thing. What we do know in these verses is that nakedness was the issue. But that speaks volumes. In the light of his sobriety, he knew there had been a sinful eye toward the nakedness of one man to another. It was abhorrent to him!

God has given us this body as a temporary dwelling in which to house His Holy Spirit while waiting for our heavenly one. The Word of God is very clear on keeping it clean, neat, in order, and in all righteousness and holiness. Could this passage about Noah in Genesis been prophetic for what was written in 2 Corinthians 5:2–4 and 10? Perhaps, as it says:

> For indeed in this house we groan, longing to be clothed with our dwelling from heaven; inasmuch as we, having put it on, shall not be found naked. For indeed while we are in this tent, we groan, being burdened, because we do not want to be unclothed, but to be clothed,

> in order that what is mortal may be swallowed up by life. For we must all appear before the judgment seat of Christ, that each one may be recompensed *for his deeds in the body*, according to what he has done, whether good or bad.

It is assured by our Divine Creator that we shall give an account of how we handle our bodies, whether for good or evil. This isn't just about sexuality. It's also about drugs, alcohol, overeating, smoking, overworking, never resting, and a vast array of other areas that take their toll upon the temple—our bodies, as given by God. Every single act committed against it will be accounted for according to the above scripture. Are your eyes and heart open to see and receive these things?

Purity Inside and Out

The Lord looks to see purity on the inside *and* on the outside. The very garments we wear are to be appropriate and distinguishable from that of the world. By that I mean, that many of the world's fashion designers don't have a clue as to what's proper or appropriate apparel for a man or woman of God. Why would they? They're looking for big profits, and that means catering to the desires of the fleshy lures of the world. This calls for a book by itself! Nonetheless, Scripture ascribes plentiful glimpses that our clothing has more accountability in God's eyes than in ours!

We must see this! If Noah became disgusted because his very garments had been tarnished with unrighteousness, it's time the men and women of God check to see if their attire is appropriate and addressed in a holy manner. Jesus' very garments were changed at the Transfiguration, and that signifies just how much God desires His people to be clothed in holiness and purity. We must have insight to the passage in Matthew 22:1–14 where a man is expelled from the Lord's presence because he is not dressed in proper wedding attire. Jesus calls him "friend" because it's His desire that none perish (2 Peter 3:9). Hallelujah! Nevertheless, He had to pass judgment on this man because of his presumptive arrogance toward holiness and God's laws, even to the degree of how he was clothed. As the saga of mankind comes to a close as shown in Revelation, we find repeated references about robes of righteousness! Revelation 22:14 says, "Blessed are those who wash their robes that they may have the right to the tree of life, and may enter by the gates into the city."

Messengers of Fire

I want to give a personal testimony here regarding something quite strange, yet profoundly amazing that happened to a close friend and me. We had gone over to a mutual friend's home to pray for her as she was very ill with a terminal disease. She was married and had children. But she had discovered a few years earlier her husband was involved in homosexuality. It crushed her heart. But they seemed to have worked through it before she became gravely ill. As my friend and I prayed for her we entered into deep, spiritual warfare and left that evening feeling as though we'd touched the very gates of heaven!

When her husband came home that night, he saw two burn marks on their driveway, as if there had been some kind of a fire on the pavement. The fire marks were circular and strange looking to be sure. He wondered at the time what it might have been, but forgot about it until the next day when a workman also saw the fire marks on the pavement. Later, two different neighbors approached him asking who those two people were standing next to the big bonfire on their driveway the night before. He was stunned! He simply had no explanation at all.

We later came to believe those two "people" must have been *messengers of fire*—angels on assignment! (Ps. 104:4; Zech. 5:3–4; Heb. 1:7). We weren't sure exactly what that assignment may have been. Nevertheless, the Lord began to open the eyes of my understanding of what those unexplained "pillars of fire" may have represented.

Sadly, our precious friend died later on, and her husband and children moved away. Nonetheless, the impact of some of our prayers may never be fully known until we get to heaven.

God miraculously protected the Hebrew children from Pharaoh as He led them out of Egypt with a pillar of fire (Gen. 13:21–22; 14:19, 20, 24)! The prophet Nehemiah recounts that amazing time, "Thou in Thy great compassion, didst not forsake them in the wilderness; the pillar of cloud did not leave them by day, to guide them on their way, nor the *pillar of fire by night*, to light for them the way in which they were to go" (Neh. 9:19). Had God in His divine strategy and sovereignty been protecting and guiding my friend and me through the mines of demonic, spiritual warfare? I believe so! Such is the danger of the atmosphere created with homosexuality.

Understanding

As my understanding of this unusual fire began to unfold, the Lord directed me to the passage in scripture regarding Sodom and Gomorrah (Gen. 19). God had sent two angels to warn Lot of what was to come and to get him out of the city before it would be burned. But as the evening hours lingered, the men of the city came to Lot's door and tried to force their way in to take the two visiting men (angels) and have sex with them. Most people know the outcome. The city burned, but not before Lot was entangled in an angry mob that was bent on engaging in homosexuality. He frantically pleaded, "Please, my brothers, do not act wickedly." And then shockingly, he offered the crowd his two daughters "who have not had relations." As horrific as that sounds, the sin of homosexuality was more abhorrent to him than even the rape of his two precious, virgin daughters!

We see similarly in Judges 19:22–24:

> "While they were making merry, behold, the men of the city, certain worthless fellows, surrounded the house, pounding on the door; and they spoke to the owner of the house, the old man, saying, 'Bring out the man who came into your house that we may have relations with him.' Then the man, the owner of the house, went out to them and said to them, 'No, my fellows, please do not act so wickedly; since this man has come into my house, do not commit this act of folly. Here is my virgin daughter and his concubine. Please let me bring them out that you may ravish them

> and do to them whatever you wish. But do not commit such an act of folly against this man.'"

Protected!

How can this be? There can be only one explanation. Relations between two people of the same sex is such a degradation to God Almighty, such a transgression of anything normal and so far past His holy ordained ways, that it called for drastic measures. This ought to tell us something!

I believe God sent angels to stand guard outside the home of this couple that night my friend and I had been making intercession. Truly, angels were sent as reinforcements as we prayed for a dying woman who had been sorely tested in her soul as had Lot. Her marriage may have still been on the brink for all we know. But the angels were there to give us a covering! They were there to protect us! The sin of homosexuality is such an abomination to God that He has in fact destroyed whole cities because of it.

Could this have played a part in the destruction of New Orleans by Hurricane Katrina where such degradation occurs during Mardi Gras? One can only speculate. But that's not to say God the Father isn't full of mercy and grace. There no such thing as 'selective love' with Him who is love! He loves all of us. And we must love as He loves. We must forgive as He forgives. Mercy triumphs over judgment for those who come running into the Savior's outstretched arms (James 2:13; Heb. 4:16). But you surrender to His will and to His ways.

Friends, we must be awakened to the earth's fading existence as the Final Judgment Day nears. *Persecution will come because purification is imminent!* There will not be many left who stand for righteousness, because it's going to cost them everything!

> Enter by the narrow gate; for the gate is wide and the way is broad that leads to destruction, and many are those who enter by it. For the gate is small and the way is narrow that leads to life and few are those who find it.
>
> —Matthew 7:13–14

Which path will you choose? Will it be the one with least resistance? Or will you take the "high way" of holiness? (Isa. 35:8).

Prayer

> *Gracious Lord Jesus, I come and bow down at Your feet. Take me as I am and cleanse me from all unrighteousness. Purify my heart according to Psalm 51. Strengthen me for every battle I face, that You may be lifted up and glorified. Prepare my heart in all purity of purpose to forgive as You forgive, to love as You love. Amen.*

◆ eight ◆

CONFUSION

MASS HYSTERIA IS coming upon the earth. It's inevitable as the end-time battle for the bride ebbs ever closer. Nonetheless, hope is alive and well in God's ordained promises! His enduring love seals our glorious fate if we're abiding in Him. The prophet Isaiah declares:

> The earth will be completely laid waste and completely despoiled, for the Lord has spoken this word. The earth mourns and withers, the world fades and withers, the exalted of the people of the earth fade away. The earth is polluted by its inhabitants, for they transgressed laws, violated statutes, broke the everlasting covenant. Therefore a curse devours the earth, and those who live in it are held guilty. Therefore the inhabitants of the earth are burned, and few men are left.
>
> —Isaiah 24:3–6

We witnessed Hurricane Katrina in the southern United States in 2005 that overwhelmed thousands of people with much confusion, chaos, uncertainty, and lawlessness. There was a sense of bitter hopelessness. Then as Hurricane Rita rode in on its coattails, it brought new levels of insecurity.

I couldn't help but note a few comments by a TV reporter who remarked as they went down flooded streets by boat, that he'd noticed a clock at a funeral home. It had stopped when the hurricane hit. It appears an alarm is being sounded loud and clear. How much *time* do we really have? Many precious people are being jarred loose from their comfortable lifestyles and thrown into the unknown. Decisions for life and death are going to have to be made quickly.

We're now entering a countdown for the final war of mankind, being catapulted toward the last hour before Jesus returns. We're being shaken and awakened to the fact that Jesus is certainly coming a second time just as He declared. Likewise, when He rose on the third day at the Resurrection, everything changed, even calendars! Once again, everything is about to be altered. But we're also on the precipice of a victorious eschatology! The gates of hell shall not prevail against the Lamb's Bride, the church (Matt. 16:18).

AWAKE!

The Lord has many wake-up calls in various ways and degrees. Please understand, He does not cause disaster, but does allow them. God's love can take what the enemy means for evil and turn it to good for those whose hearts are surrendered to Him. What a glorious hope (Gen. 50:20)! Nonetheless, is anyone answering those wake-up calls? Is anyone discerning the signs of the times? Is anyone listening? How is it we can look at a dark sky and discern that a storm is approaching, but we can't discern the times that we have now entered? We must take to heart the Lord's admonition about our lack of fortitude and knowledge of these things (Matt.

16:1–4). In this chapter Jesus says the only sign some will have will be the sign of Jonah, who was in the deep, dark recesses of the belly of the whale for three days and three nights representing the Lord's three day scenario of death and Resurrection. Deep darkness is coming upon the earth, but so is great light (Isa. 60)! We ought to be comforted we've been given a little more time. We're being urged with more opportunities than ever to come to know who we are in the bosom of the Most High God.

Sadly, some of the most horrific casualties on the heels of Hurricane Katrina came with Hurricane Rita when a busload of elderly people were burned to death in a terrible accident. We grieve for those who were lost in these tragedies. But we must understand we're closing in on a time when many kinds of disasters will be unleashed. You and I will need to have our hearts comforted and melted in the passionate pursuit of the Prince of Peace, Jesus Christ. This will afford us survival and victory in the most trying of times. "Now may the God of Peace Himself sanctify you entirely; and may your spirit and soul and body be preserved complete, without blame at the coming of our Lord Jesus Christ" (1 Thess. 5:23; Isa. 9:6; Rev. 3:16). Accelerated change is on the horizon.

Confusion will deepen as mankind insists on its own ways in total rebellion against God. At its deepest root, rebellion is simply not knowing who we are in Christ Jesus and that we have been ordained to be His eternal Bride. The battle is raging, and seemingly out of control. Demonic fires are raging all across the earth and the smoke is bringing a stench into the very nostrils of God (Amos 4:10).

Decisions

Decisions will have to be made quickly in the coming days, as there may be only a split second to choose "this day who we will serve" (Josh. 24:15). We will have to decide which corridor to take, just as many survivors had to on September 11, 2001. Confusion as to who we and what we're made of may hang in the balance. Which way will we go? God's way or ours? Do we belong to the most High God? Or do we take ownership of ourselves, suffering eternal consequences?

This is the eleventh hour! We've entered the finality of humanity. The Old Testament book of Judges is ringing loud and clear across the land: "In those days, there was no king in Israel. Everyone did what was right in their eyes" (Judg. 17:6). We're bombarded daily in our newspapers, magazines, radio talk shows, TV, movies, and other areas of society with acceptance of people's 'alternative' lifestyles. The mantra of the hour is, "If it feels good, do it!" Again, the eternal question of the first garden looms nearby, "Did God really say…?" The heart of Father God cries out to the lost and dying world!

Confusion

Satan is the author of confusion and he masterminds it well (1 Cor. 14:33). How confusing can it be for our precious children to have two daddies or two mommies when scripture clearly states otherwise? How confusing can it be for a child to bring friends into the home and introduce their new mom who used to be a man and was their dad, but is now a woman but still married to their mom? I saw this very thing on Oprah Winfrey one day! I can hardly say it, let alone comprehend it.

How confusing can it be when a famous former men's basketball star shows up in a wedding dress for a publicity interview? How confusing can it be for a child in a homosexual/lesbian home to know what clothes to put on for school each morning? How confusing can it be to wonder which locker room you're supposed to be in or which public restroom to use? How confusing can it be when cosmetic counters are showing lipstick for men, touting gender neutral makeup? And how in the world are the children of this complex generation going to know who they are in such an atmosphere of confusion, deceit, and sin? Has the entire world gone mad? Probably. Now they are trying to have a court declare a chimpanzee as a person![1]

Freedom

Where does it stop? It doesn't. The reason is that a delusional lie of who we are called to be has been released across the globe. Take note of Galatians 5:1 that says it was for freedom that Christ set us free and that we are not to be subject to a yoke of slavery, doing things are own way. Living righteously is very freeing. It's really very simple! We must remember that God is not a God of confusion. Satan is the author of confusion!

Quite frankly, it's not about religion, it's about relationship with our Creator Jehovah God. Anyone can have religion. But far too often, in the façade of religion, this relationship is the missing element. There needs to be the saving ingredient of communion and fellowship with the Lord Jesus Christ. The heart of the matter is our up-close and personal encounters with Him. Religion can be void of His presence and power according to Mark 7:6–7:

> This people honors Me with their lips, but their heart is far away from Me. But in *vain* do they worship Me, teaching as doctrines the precepts of men.

Our Children

Our precious children must decide matters of soul and spirit at an earlier age than ever before. The soul engages things of the flesh along with soulish issues involving spiritual demonic activity. One example is the Harry Potter phenomena, by which so many of our young ones have been enticed. A heart engaged with the Holy Spirit operates from the heavenly, higher perspectives of His nature of holiness and purity (Heb. 4:12). The Bible says that even these very young ones can know Him personally, such as in Psalm 8:2, "From the mouth of infants and nursing babes Thou hast established strength, because of Thine adversaries, to make the enemy and the revengeful cease." (See also Matthew 11:25.) We must make sure they know the Lord Jesus.

Young and impressionable children are quickly influenced one way or the other. Nearly every day there are implications in the media to the alternate lifestyles that do not align with God's Word. Many relationships are being redefined by worldly standards, not by God. Some states are already removing the wording "man and wife" to read "married partners" in school textbooks.[1] Are we aware of what's going on in our schools? Do we not realize how subtle the enemy is? Followers of Jesus must now be on high alert as alarms are going off all across the land!

Battle lines are being drawn every day. These things are not only at the early elementary levels, but in high schools and especially colleges where there are many gay and transsexual fraternities.[2] The bombardment of these alternate lifestyles is so far out in the open, it's swallowing up those who stand for righteousness. Most would rather take the no-fuss, no-stance route. Political correctness seems to have blinded them.

Payday is coming! God has spoken and He is the final answer. We are little human beings with little breath. What does that compare to Jehovah God? Let's cry out with Job, "By the breath of God they perish, and by the blast of His anger they come to an end" (Job 4:9).

The world is raging at this very hour to take God out of everything that's ever been foundational to His people. Many in our own country are demanding we take God out of the Pledge of Allegiance to the flag. Many want the phrase "In God We Trust" taken off our money. We've already seen skirmishes involving the removal of the Ten Commandments from public places. Praying before Congress and praying at commencement exercises have also been contested. These protesters sound more like spoiled rotten children who want their own way and if they don't get it, they'll take it all the way to the Supreme Court of the land!

God's Court

God *is* the Supreme Court! And of course, it's higher than that of man. (See Daniel 7; Rev. 20:12; 21:27.) It's in session continually, handing down decrees of life and death for those who will bow or not bow to His will and to His ways. When we pull our last breath into our lungs and are instantly transported to the other side of the veil that separates the earthly realm from the eternal spiritual realm, we'll meet the Judge all right! Heaven and hell are for real. And hell is a whole lot hotter than anything of this world. Life is merely a vapor, the Bible tells us (James 4:14). Eternity is, well, eternity! Oh, the peace that resides within hearts who confidently know who they are in the Lord Jesus, having full assurance of eternal bliss with Him.

Unfortunately, the ultimate violation of God's marital laws are now being sanctioned in many countries even as I write this, for they have already approved gay and lesbian marriages. Our country may be next. We're edging dangerously close. Our nation now is in the process of opening up public schools supported with tax dollars that are specifically for gays, bisexuals, and transgenders.[3] It goes to the other spectrum as well, where many developers are now marketing retirement communities for gays and lesbians only.

Again, one has to wonder, "Where will it stop?" It won't. *The battle for the pure bride is raging hot and heavy!* Times, seasons, and epochs are rushing to a close. In the twinkling of an eye the fierce Warrior King, the Lion of Judah, will set foot on earth just as He said (Rev. 5:5). Are you ready for this? Are you ready to meet your Creator and Designer? We need to know what's in the Manufacturer's Manual (the Bible). None of us knows which breath will be our last one. There can be no question on that day or even at this very moment as to who you are. Our Divine Creator, in the First Garden, made them male and female, man and woman, husband and wife, and there can be no changing of the guard in that. Satan's desire is to invade a human heart to twist, tear, and torment it away from God's love (1 Cor. 14:33). Satan's demented purpose is to take the beauty of God's creation and distort and misalign it so there can't be praise given to the divine Designer who made them in His own image. People who will not bow before the living, eternal, Jehovah God, to His will and to His ways, will always face a vast array of confusion in their lives, never knowing who they were created to be.

Jesus asked Peter the question, "Who do you say that I am?" (Matt. 16:15–17). When Peter answers, "Thou art the Christ, the Son of the Living God," Jesus responded by telling him that flesh and blood did not bring this revelation, but His Father who is in heaven. We must understand our identity is not found through the world's eyes, but only by the power of Christ within us!

Do We Even Care?

But there is a cry in my heart, a sobbing deep within me that yearns for the freeing of the sons and daughters of God! How much more so in the Lord's own heart for those He died to redeem! Let them not be defiled by the confusion and the wicked conspiracy of the world, the flesh, and the devil. The people of God must wake up. But does anyone even care? I'm asking those of you who are holding this book in your hands—do *you* care? Oh, that we might pray for this emerging generation of young ones! It shall be they who will be tested the most. It is they who will pay the highest price to bring sacred truth to the nations as martyrdom brings revelation.

A holy convergence of the all the ages is upon us. A fight for the finish is emerging. Many are dealing with turmoil deep within their souls. Multitudes are already in the valley of decision (Joel 3:14). The young people of today will have to be like David, who as a boy came against Goliath who taunted and defied God's people.

Goliath is the world's systems and its courts. This will be their test! This will define their strength in God's holy, undiluted truth.

Are you and I upholding these things? Are we standing strong? Are we teaching our children and grandchildren to make a stand for truth? God's Word is very strong on this point of taking a bold position of holiness and righteousness:

> Fathers...bring them up in the discipline and instruction of the Lord; Stand firm against the schemes of the devil; Take up the full armor of God, that you may be able to resist in the evil day, and having done everything, to stand firm. Stand firm therefore, having girded your loins with Truth and having put on the breastplate of righteousness...
>
> —Ephesians 6:13–14

Stand up! God's calling you! He's recruiting you for His end-time army! Victory is assured!

Prayer

> *O Lord of might, power, and glory, I pray to always have strength to stand for Your eternal truths. Teach me to never compromise Your righteousness. May my heart always be on alert for the schemes of the enemy. Equip me with heavenly armor according to Ephesians 6. I praise You for my purposeful identity through the cleansing blood of Jesus. Help me to be a reflection of Your purity and holiness. Amen.*

◆ nine ◆

DESTRUCTION OR DISCERNMENT? BLOOD DONOR?

OH, THE POWER of true love! It goes to great lengths to protect its beloved! I've seen parents at the bedside of their dying children saying that they'd trade places with them if it were possible.

In life, there are all kinds of wars. As in any war, unfortunately there are casualties. Some pay the ultimate price for freedom with their very lives. In light of that, how many want to sign up for the front lines? Probably not many. But that's what is transpiring for anyone who desires to claim the slain Lamb of God as their King. If you're going to be in His kingdom, martyrdom very well could be a reality because the King's domain has been, and always will be fiercely contended (Heb. 11). Armageddon's eventual knock on our door will intensify that fight.

One day I heard the Lord ask me in my spirit, "Are you willing to be a blood donor?" I immediately thought of the Red Cross organization that promotes giving blood for their blood banks. These life-saving banks need to be kept filled so we can be prepared for all kinds of natural disasters. But, what about spiritual disasters? What about life in the eternal realm? The Lord was asking if I'd be a blood donor in a way I had not pondered. Was I willing to give my blood as a martyr that another may live spiritually in eternity? It's a sobering question to be sure. But it does follow the way of the cross of Christ! If you and I intend to fully follow Him, this may become a more pertinent question in the very near future. After all, it was He who said:

> And he who does not take up his cross and follow after Me is not *worthy* of Me. He who has found his life shall lose it, and he who has lost his life for My sake shall find it.
>
> —Matthew 10:38–39

Sound confusing? Not so. A heart surrendered to the Savior loses its sinful ways in order to gain heavenly ground. It's a good exchange!

Lovers of God are just like Him. He's a Giver, and they are, too! I love the words in Hebrews 11:38 where it says the world was not worthy of those who became martyrs for the Lord. The world does not care about such jewels, it despises them. But God sees! He knows! He cares!

A Reason for Living and Dying

Those who are bent on finding their own way, doing their own thing, and living only for themselves are in critical condition and close to losing eternal life. The current breath in our nostrils is precariously fleeting. It can be snuffed out at any given moment for any given reason. It's gone in a vapor. Compare that to a place that's never ending as heaven and hell are. Why play games with God?

When you bow to the supreme authority of God, surrendering to His eternal plan of salvation, you actually find yourself! You become a reflection of His holiness. You begin to know exactly who you are! You discover your identity and purpose in life. You find a reason for living, and for dying. Losing your life in something bigger than yourself brings you to the very point of why you were born in the first place. You were born to love the Lord your God with all your heart, mind, soul, and body, and to worship Him forever and ever! This is purity of purpose. It's the divine plan! A commitment to our heavenly Bridegroom, Jesus, aligns you with the fact that it is no longer you who lives, but Christ who lives in you! And the life you now live in the flesh, you "live by the faith in the Son of God" who loves you and delivered Himself up for you as stated in Galatians 2:20. As in an earthly marriage, the Bride of Christ becomes one in the bond of love with Him. It's similar to the vows taken in an earthly marriage where one makes the commitment, "for better, for worse, for richer, for poorer, in sickness and in health, till death" when you meet your God face to face!

The Mark—The Wedding Ring

This spiritual commitment to honor the sacrificial blood of the Lamb of God puts a holy mark upon your soul. His saving blood becomes your wedding ring, so to speak. It's a mark of pure commitment to the profound ways of a holy, righteous God. Acceptance of our heavenly Bridegroom's atonement is cause for great celebration! "Do not harm the earth or the sea or the trees, until we have sealed the bond-servants of our God on their foreheads" (Rev. 6:3; 9:4). This godly mark is like no other. Its significance will be especially evident in the day of the Lord. It will distinguish them from all the peoples of the earth.

It will shine brilliantly through those who belong to the Most High God. Not Muhammad, not Allah, but the most high God! Jehovah! The great "I AM." The Alpha, Omega, the Beginning, the End, the Eternal One who was, is, and is to come again! The one who changes not (Mal. 3:6; Rev. 1:8)!

As the latter days come, we'll see no shortage of those with contrary natures of rebellion and unrighteousness. We're told in Matthew 7:13 the road to destruction is wide and many take that route. Why? Because human nature has a tendency to follow the crowd, dress alike, look alike, act alike, be like everyone else, go with the majority. Many are afraid of standing out in the pack, preferring not to make waves. I really love what Pastor Bill Johnson from Redding, California, recently said, "Be a wave maker!" Go for it! Be brave![1]

No Blushing

Deep darkness is seeping into our lives (Isa. 60:1–3). Horrendous evil such as has never been known before is edging ever closer into men's hearts who have not taken the heavenly Bridegroom as their King. It's hard to imagine or even describe the evil now being perpetrated in this hour in which we live. As I began writing this book and doing research, I started a file of unbelievably evil things being reported through the media. That file began to grow far too fast and was most sickening.

One story involved a man who went by way of the Internet to find someone who would be willing to be killed by him so he could eat their flesh. This man said it wasn't that he wanted to know what murdering someone might feel like, but that he wanted to know a kind of intimacy with another man in the manner of eating his body. Is this not beyond utter shock? It's beyond comprehension, to say the least. Just as shocking, was the number of people who responded to this demented man's request. To be honest, it's time to throw that file out of my office!

These demonic shock waves continue day after day in the media bringing exposure of these evil deeds for not only our children to see, but people everywhere in this global society. This is of the utmost sorrow because our young, impressionable children are the ones who will lead the next generation. How shall they lead if they've been desensitized, seeing little compassion, very little integrity or honor, grace, humility, or godly love? How shall they lead if they don't even know how to blush? Jeremiah prophesied centuries ago:

> To whom shall I speak and give warning that they may hear? Behold their ears are closed and they cannot listen. Behold the word of the Lord has become a reproach to them; they have no delight in it. From the least of them even to the greatest of them, everyone is greedy for gain, and from the prophet even to the priest everyone deals falsely. And they have healed the brokenness of My people superficially, saying, 'Peace, peace,' but there is no peace. Were they ashamed because of the abomination they have done? They were not even ashamed at all; *they did not even know how to blush.*
>
> —Jeremiah 6:10, 13–15, emphasis added

UNCONTROLLED

The world's lusts, spurred on by satanic escalation, have now entered the Last Days of uncontrolled passions and unbridled constraints where just about anything goes. Forget the consequences. Are we aware of these things? Are we blind, deaf, numb, and dumb? Is anyone alive out there? Is anyone awake? Generations up to this point in time had some guidelines, but this one seems to be throwing all caution to the wind.

Daniel enlightens us to these things in 8:23–25:

> And in the latter period of their rule, when the transgressors have run their course, a king will arise insolent and skilled in intrigue. And his power will be mighty, but not by his own power, and he will destroy to an extraordinary degree and prosper and perform his will; He will destroy mighty men and the holy people. And through his shrewdness He will cause deceit to succeed by his influence; and he will magnify himself in his heart, and he will destroy many while they are at ease. He will even oppose the Prince of princes, but he will be broken without human agency.

As the fiercest battle of the ages looms closer, the distinct nature of God's people will become more evident. But there will be precious few of them! More than at any other time in history, they'll pay a costly price to follow the Lord. Forget homes and lands, it's going to come down to their very lives! The world has become extremely intolerant of anything pure or holy. Sadly, this is true even in some houses of worship. But judgment will *start* there. Far too many are failing to uphold God's commandments. Compromise has crept in to a dangerous degree (Deut. 32:36; Heb. 10:30). A mark is being distributed to everyone on earth for eternal destruction or eternal life. It's an on-going spiritual process that will conclude at the Lord's Second Appearing. Which mark do you have?

Confidence

What choices are you making right now? Are you self-absorbed in making your own way? Are you straddling too many fences, compromising too many things? Are you so lukewarm you couldn't imagine what passionate desire for God really is? Are you aware of your need for His mark on your heart so you can truly live a life of power and purity? Do you know you need a Savior? We all do!

Jesus wants us to enter into fellowship with Him through His shed blood on the Cross. There is power in that *red cross*! As the old song goes, "There is power, power, wonder working power in the precious Blood of the Lamb!"[2] This is the only way to inherit freedom from our sinful bondages. He wants us to abide in Him that we may be holy and pure in our mind, soul, and body.

> Since therefore, brethren, we have confidence to enter the holy place by the blood of Jesus, by a new and living way which He inaugurated for us through the veil, that is His flesh, and since we have a great priest over the house of God, let us draw near with a sincere heart in full assurance of faith, having our hearts sprinkled clean from an evil conscience and our bodies washed with pure water. Let us hold fast the confession of our hope without wavering, for He who promised is faithful.
>
> —Hebrews 10:19–23

When Armageddon appears, there will be no fear in those committed to Christ. They will be like Shadrach, Meshach, and Abednego in Daniel 3 who were threatened with martyrdom if they would not bow to the ungodly king Nebuchadnezzar and worship his false gods. These fiercely committed men of God boldly stood their ground defying the king's orders, thus bringing certain death. Nevertheless, they testified that Almighty God was able to deliver them from this horrendous fate. Some of the most powerful words in the Bible are found in this passage when they went even further by telling the king that *even if God did not deliver them*, they still would never bow in worship to the golden image! Integrity of heart to God's ordained ways is the only path to eternal fellowship with Him, no matter what the cost. They were willing to be blood donors.

In the Lord's holy love, nothing but sin can separate us from Him—tribulation can't, nor distress, persecution, famine, nor death, life, angels, principalities, nor things present or things to come, nor height, nor depth, nor any other created thing, as stated in Romans 8:31–39. If God is for us, who can be against us?

Spiritual Emergency Room

A compromised lifestyle is a dangerous lifestyle. Spiritually speaking, it's living near the brink of spiritual death. There may be no time to go to an ER at church. There may be no time to call for a specialist in your pastor. There may be no time to utter a prayer for forgiveness of violating God's ordained laws. If you were in a car accident, plane crash, experienced a terrorist attack, or whatever might precipitate an instantaneous moment of conscious time on this side of the natural and supernatural realms, compromise means you are in spiritual critical condition!

As earth's last days come, lukewarm hearts will grow cool, colder, and then deathly cold: "And because lawlessness is increased, most people's love will grow cold" (Matt. 24:12). Many people simply do not have the fire for God! Passion to know, serve, and love Him deeply is missing in their lives. More often than not, they do not ascribe to His higher ways of holiness, preferring their own ways instead (Isa. 55:8–9). The end of the story reveals, "So because you are lukewarm, and neither hot nor cold, I will spit you out of my mouth" (Rev. 3:16). Who wants that? Take the Lord for all He's worth! He has so much to offer us all. It's a matter of bowing one's entire being to King Jesus that we may have abundant life with righteous power (John 10:10).

Great trials now await us. The lifeblood of the Lamb of God must run through our spiritual veins so we'll be equipped to discern matters at hand. Just as the hypocritical spirit of religion was present in Jesus' day, so it is again. It's making great inroads around the earth. Briefly, here's a look at the dangerous religious spirit:

- More concerned with the *acts* of religion than an authentic, humble relationship with God
- Works oriented and preoccupied with star performance
- Legalistic and rigid
- Judgmental and condescending
- Prideful
- Conformity-oriented
- Glorifies self; does not point to God alone

- Concerned with their gifts and the display of them
- Seeks the favor of men more than that of God
- Contains some truth, but is out of balance
- Often unteachable, thinking they know it all
- Controlling and authoritarian
- Flees accountability

This contaminating religious spirit, seen especially through the Pharisees of Jesus' day, will bring vicious attacks upon the Bride of Christ as His Second Coming nears. "They will make you outcasts from the synagogue, but an hour is coming for everyone who kills you to think that he is offering service to God" (John 16:2; see also Matt. 23 and John 12:37–43).

Be aware. Be alert. Be watchful. Do not be deceived. Religious spirits are depriving many of the holy, ordained relationship they are to have with the Son of God:

> For the time will come when they will not endure sound doctrine; but wanting to have their ears tickled, they will accumulate for themselves teachers in accordance to their own desires; and will turn away their ears from the truth and will turn aside to myths.
>
> —2 Timothy 4:3–4

In our own country, our "Battle Hymn of the Republic" speaks plainly of the free flow of righteous blood! The last stanza reads:[3]

In the beauty of the lilies,
Christ was born across the sea,
With a glory in His bosom
That transfigures you and me;
As He died to make men holy,
Let us live to make men free,
While God is marching on!

These prophetic words are going to take on a whole new meaning in the future. Yes, die for the honor of your country. But how much more so for the honor of the King of kings and Lord of lords!

> Worship the Lord in holy attire; tremble before Him, all the earth…He will judge the peoples with equity.
>
> —Psalm 96:9–10

Diluted

We need to be prepared for the impending Armageddon. It's upon us. We must be discerning of lukewarm, compromising, weak, whitewashed souls who twist ears with diluted truths from God's Word, causing it to be useless and powerless in thousands of lives:

> For certain persons have crept in unnoticed, those who were long beforehand marked out for this condemnation, ungodly persons who turn the grace of our God into licentiousness and deny our only Master and Lord, Jesus Christ.
>
> —Jude 4

The rebellious acts of unrighteous civil courts worldwide are now making judgments contrary to the Word of God, declaring marriages to be legal between persons of the same sex. They've "turned justice into poison, and the fruit of righteousness into wormwood" (Amos 6:12).

The New Testament book of Jude informs us how God judged angels who did not keep their holy domain. If angels were judged, how much more so earthlings who commit abominations:

> ...just as Sodom and Gomorrah and the cities around them, since they in the same way as these indulged in gross immorality and went after strange flesh, are exhibited as an example, in undergoing the punishment of eternal fire. Yet in the same manner these men, also by dreaming, defile the flesh and reject authority, and revile angelic majesties.
>
> —Jude 1:6–7

God's Word is very clear on these matters. Jude states it even stronger in verses 18–19, "In the last time there shall be mockers, following after their own ungodly lusts. These are the ones who cause divisions, worldly-minded, devoid of the Spirit." We need to examine ourselves according to God's Word to see if we are indeed *devoid* of His Spirit. The question needs to be answered—now.

Prayer

My God, King, and Savior Jesus, I profess my undying love for You. As You gave Your life for me, I give my life to You in its entirety that I may live with You forever. Help me to discern Your true paths of righteousness. I will wear the wedding band of the cross in my heart forevermore. Amen.

◆ ten ◆

GOD'S WORD, A HOT COMMODITY

THERE IS A romance of God's Word coming! People are going to begin to fall passionately in love with the Bible. Exuberant joy will be heard throughout the land!

Jehovah's Word is the last word on every matter known to mankind. It is the final authority in the end, as well as the beginning. His divine courts will override and overrule every earthly court system in the end. Everything will stand or fall according to His Word alone. Why? Because it's His *breath*, His *Ruwach* (Hebrew for breath).[1] His movement, His power, His authority, His reign, His rule, and His Eternal Word! He's God and we are not. He speaks and things just are! God said, "Let there be…" and it was so (Genesis 1). His divine Word is the criteria for judging the matters of men. It ought to make us tremble with holy, reverential fear.

Gloriously, His Word is about to become the hottest commodity on earth as it was purposed to be since it was first spoken to a human being on Day Six of Creation. It's about to sear through the conscience of every heart like a red-hot iron! This searing will be for better or for worse depending on obedience or disobedience to His revealed written Word in the Bible.

I love how God talks to us! He not only speaks through the Holy Scriptures, but also through the beauty of His creation in nature, people, events in our lives, even through dreams. But we must always be certain that His written Word can confirm everything. If something does *not* align itself to biblical standards, than it simply is not of God.

Dreams

For the moment, I'm going to address the way the Lord uses dreams. Everyone has them. People like talking about them especially if they have caused an alteration in their lives. Perhaps someone was considering a different school, job, or whom to marry and they've had a dream that makes them rethink their decision. From time to time you hear of these kinds of revelations, and it's quite amazing to say the least. How many of you have had significant dreams that you've remembered for years? Some dreams can be recurring, haunting, or foreboding with warnings. What do you do with them? Do you pay any attention to them or just brush them off?

Since everyone has dreams, it's wise to scrutinize them. They often send messages to us, for better or worse, either through nightmares by the demonic world, in which case they should be immediately deleted from our memory, or they're for revelation and direction from the Lord. People are paying closer attention to their dreams. It's become somewhat of a fascination to the world, but also to the church. Many are attending dream seminars or taking courses on symbols, interpretations, and the language of dreams.

It's of great interest right now, which is not surprising since the Old Testament book of Joel says:

> And it will come about after this that I will pour out My Spirit on all mankind; and your sons and daughters will prophesy, your old men will dream dreams, your young men will see visions.
>
> —Joel 2:28

God has used this mechanism of the subconscious mind to speak to people all through the ages. In the opening book of the Bible, Genesis 20 shows us King Abimelech being warned by the Lord in a dream that he would be a dead man if he has relations with Sarah, Abraham's wife. The king was about to commit adultery and die for it! Of course, Abraham had lied to the king about her true identity in order to save his own skin! But the king had been in the dark, so to speak, until this experience. He gave her back to her husband and his life was spared. Dreams can be powerful!

This first biblically recorded dream comes immediately on the heels of the immoral events of homosexuality in Sodom and Gomorrah, and the incest in Lot's family in Genesis 19. These cities were given a warning through an angel of the Lord, but died because of their hardness of heart. They suffered the consequence that King Abimelech avoided.

We must understand that God's love is so passionate for us He will go to any lengths to capture our attention! Dreams will do that. From Joseph in Genesis 37, to the book of Daniel, to Joseph in the New Testament in Matthew 1, throughout the Bible, dreams have been powerfully used by the Lord to direct mankind. He will continue to do so until the closure of earthly existence, just as the prophet Joel stated.

A Personal Dream

I wanted to lay that brief foundation because of a dream I'm going to share with you. A while ago, I had a dream that was brief, yet very graphic, and shook me to the core. As I pondered it, I knew the Lord had made it clear I was to share it with the church and whomever would listen and take heed. Precarious days lie ahead for all of us, and we must literally fall in love with God's written Word in order to survive.

In this dream I could see many people outside a movie theatre lining up. It appeared that whatever was showing must be something really fantastic because of the size of the crowds waiting in long lines to get in. In the next moment, I saw the inside of the theatre. Not one seat was left empty as it was packed to capacity. Suddenly I heard people squealing with excitement as they "oohed" and "ahhed" at what they were watching on the big screen. They were simply amazed, almost in shock and awe of what they were seeing! Upon closer observation, I could see the Word of God in huge letters on the theatre screen. But the letters were so preposterously huge you could only see a portion of one single word of Scripture. Yet the crowds were thrilled with it!

I would liken this scene to something of that in a doctor's office where they use an eye chart to check your vision. The first line on those charts is usually quite large and consists of perhaps just one or two letters of the alphabet.

That's how the Word of God appeared in this dream. These gigantic letters, showing only a portion of one word from the Bible, appeared to be the thrill of a lifetime for those at this show! Amazingly, everyone seemed able to finish the Word, knowing what it was because they *knew* it by divine revelation. This is exactly what it says in Luke 24:45, "Then He opened their minds to understand the scriptures." In the dream, those in the theatre were simply stunned by the wonder, power, and glory of it! It was truly a spectacle to see. I was filled with much joy and amazement that *this* was the main attraction!

Dear friends, people are going to begin coming out in droves to see the Word of God. In this dream, it was the talk of the town! Oh, what love for the Bible is about to emerge! God's Word was showing, being made manifest through many signs, wonders, and miracles. It was utterly spectacular. It was as if people were watching some great action adventure as gasps of breathless wonder filled the room. The looks on their faces was of sheer delight. I remember feeling so happy in the dream that people had awakened to the majesty and splendor of the Holy Scripture. Many were falling in love with Him. A love story was showing!

Interpretation

The meaning is clear. Listen! The Lord wants us to know we are now entering a time where His Word will manifest and be seen in ways beyond our wildest dreams. He declares, "The latter glory of this house will be greater than the former" (Hag. 2:9). This is what we've been waiting for! We are about to enter into the latter glory of God's people on earth. The miracles, signs, wonders, and healings of the Bible are about to be magnified and multiplied to an astounding degree. This will bring forth a reverential fear of the Lord over every nation, bringing in an unprecedented harvest of souls at the end of the age. Many will ask Him to be their Savior, but unbelievably, many will also curse Him (Rev. 16:9)! I remember a few years ago while in prayer, the Lord said, "Pray they accept the miracles!" I didn't understand it then. I do now.

Beware also of the signs of false gods and the religious spirits of the world. They too shall perform wonders, just as the magicians in Moses' day. However, it was the staff of Moses that swallowed up the other magician's serpents (Exod. 7:8–13)! Likewise, the end times will fulfill these words of prophecy from Revelation 16:13–15:

> And I saw coming out of the mouth of the dragon and out of the mouth of the beast and out of the mouth of the false prophet, three unclean spirits like frogs; for they are the spirits of demons, performing signs, which go out to the kings of the whole world, to gather them together for *the war of the great day of God* the Almighty. Behold, I am coming like a thief. Blessed is the one who stays awake and keeps his garments, lest he walk about naked and men see his shame. And they gathered them together to the place which in Hebrew is called Har-Magedon [Armageddon].

There is only one God, one Word, one divine revelation for the redemption of man, and it is through the Word made flesh, the sacrificed Lamb of God, Jesus Christ. Anything unclean cannot tolerate the holy truths of God's revealed Word. Remember that. Because at the end of the age, there will be many delusional theories floating around.

God's breath ever moves throughout mankind. Many will catch it as a radio wave, receiving it in their hearts. They'll be gloriously saved from God's judgments, delivered from sin and sickness. They will fall deeply, passionately in love with His divine Word. They will begin to devour it day and night. It will be their sustenance, victory, and joy! God's Word is living, and as it has always been, ever shall it be (Ps. 119). We would be wise to follow the Manufacturer's Manual. It reminds me how, often as I'm preparing dinner, if I don't follow a new recipe thoroughly, my dish may not turn out as well as I would hope. Those who use God's recipe, His Word, are assured of success leading to eternal life.

Jehovah's words in the Bible are blowing across the earth powerfully upon many hearts in this precarious hour of humanity. It's as though it's picking up speed as all the generations and ages are culminating (Heb. 11:39–40; 12:1–3). Divine acceleration is taking place! The Lord is about to send forth His reaping angels from the four corners of the earth as He descends from on high to take His holy bride away to be with Him forever.

> And He will send forth His angels with a great trumpet and they will gather together His elect from the four winds, from one end of the sky to the other.
>
> —Matthew 24:31

Devoid of the Spirit of God!

Multitudes will see the manifest Word of God through many holy miracles, signs and wonders, and yet, just like Pharaoh, they will not believe in the Lord Jesus because of their stone, cold hearts (Matt. 24:12). These are the ones who will read into God's Word what they choose. They will treat the Bible like an infomercial on TV, slicing, dicing, and mixing it to match their own philosophies. They want to write the chapters of their own lives in their own way—but the King of kings, who has the final say, will write the last chapter. His kingdom will come and be established on earth as it is in heaven.

> For certain persons have crept in unnoticed, those who were long beforehand marked out for this condemnation, ungodly persons who turn the grace of God into licentiousness and deny our only Master and Lord, Jesus Christ…Just as Sodom and Gomorrah and the cities around them, since they in the same way as these indulged in gross immorality and went after strange flesh, are exhibited as an example in undergoing the punishment of eternal fire. Yet in the same manner these men, also by dreaming, defile the flesh, and reject authority, and revile angelic majesties.
>
> —Jude 1:4, 7–8

Those whose hearts are joined with the Lord will be the only ones allowed in God's kingdom. Anything else is an abomination worthy of eternal damnation as stated in the Bible.

Alarms are going off everywhere. Do you hear them? Courts are in session around the globe deciding issues that have already been set in the eternal pattern of an Almighty, everlasting God who changes not. The New Testament book of Jude cautions, "In the last time there shall be mockers, following after their own ungodly lusts. These are the ones who cause divisions, worldly-minded, devoid of the Spirit" (Jude 1:18–19).

Many parade around as being aligned with the Lord Jesus and His Word, but are in fact a cheap imitation proclaiming a diluted message of the Gospel. They profess Christ, but wear the mask of deception:

> These men are those who are hidden reefs in your love feasts when they feast with you without fear, caring for themselves; clouds without water, carried along by winds; autumn trees without fruit, doubly dead, uprooted; wild waves of the sea, casting up their own shame like foam; wandering stars, for whom the black darkness has been reserved forever.
>
> —Jude 1:12–13

God's Word is not a mix-master of mush. It's very plain to see where His line is drawn and where man's flesh is. One cannot toy with the inscrutable power and authority as the eternal Godhead. Submitting in all sincerity to Him by confessing our sins affords us eternal bliss with Him forever. It's the ultimate love story! And like my dream of the theatre, many will begin to fall in love with God's Word, being awed and overcome by it. Passion to know what He has to say will invade their souls. People everywhere are growing weary of this world's wasted ways of living. They're tired, worn out, and ready to call it quits. But the Lord anxiously and tenderly waits for them to call upon His name so that they can be saved.

These dear hearts will know the joy of the Lord beyond anything this world can offer.

Hot Commodity

People are being weighed eternally by how they handle the Word of God. The Lord assures us, "All Scripture is God breathed and profitable for teaching, for reproof, for correction, for training in righteousness" (2 Tim. 3:16). Jehovah's breath has been flowing and blowing over many peoples across the ages and generations. It's alive—ever breathing, ever moving, ever accomplishing the purposes for which it was sent (Isa. 55:11).

Have you ever had someone get right in your face when they're talking to you, so close that you actually feel their breath? This is exactly what God wants us to experience every time we read the Bible. It's not just about reading the scriptures, it's the up-close and personal encounter one has with Him while reading it. How can this be? Because when His Word is released into your life, you cannot read the scriptures and stay the same. You'll either progress if you accept it, or you'll regress if you reject it.

God's breath always stirs, changes, shifts, and alters things—significantly. Why? Because He's God, it's His breath, and His Word. Nothing can stay the same:

> For the Word of God is living and active and sharper than any two-edged sword and piercing as far as the division of soul and spirit; of both joints and marrow, and able to judge the thoughts and intentions of the heart.
>
> —Hebrews 4:12

This era of humanity will be a time of unprecedented movement of God, not unlike the first Pentecost (Acts 2). The fire of conviction is going to be turned up to a greater degree. It's going to bring people to a point of decision, one way or the other. They'll have to accept it or reject it for what it is—truth. There will be a new sense, a new revelation of the power emanating from I AM's written Word. He declares to us through Jeremiah, "Is not My Word like fire?" (Jer. 23:29). That heat brings *awareness*. Where there's fire, there's light. Something truly emanates from His Word. The word *emanate* is described in the dictionary as "issue." It *is* an issue! It also means "originate." It is the origin! The other meaning is "flow out." And it will more than ever!

Dramatically Affected

I believe there could be a time when anyone who even walks within the perimeter of a Bible will be dramatically affected. They might be in a coffee shop where someone is studying it, or where a student may have one in a school locker. Maybe they'll be walking in a shopping mall, restaurant, hotel, or by someone's desk at work, or wherever a Bible may be placed, and they will sense something is happening. They'll take note of it with curses or praise!

One of the reasons God's Word will become such a hot commodity is that nations, tribes, and tongues are looking for supernatural answers to their dilemmas as the world gets darker. People are actually beginning to look beyond themselves either rightfully or wrongfully, but at least they're *looking*! Many are about to discover the Word of God is the final answer to their dilemma as well as the grand finale, "Heaven and earth will pass away, but My words shall not pass away" (Matt. 24:35).

Jesus is coming again. He is the final authority. He is the Word made flesh and He dwelt among us (John 1). He became the sacrificial Lamb of God that we might be cleansed, washed, and set free from all sin and all disease.

Remember my dream that I shared at the beginning of this chapter? Know this: God's Word is showing near you. Do you see it? Do you feel it? What will you do with it?

Some of the very last few words of Scripture read:

> I testify to everyone who hears the words of the prophecy of this book: if anyone adds to them, God shall add to him the plagues which are written in this book; and if anyone takes away from the words of the book of this prophecy, God shall take away his part from the tree of life and from the holy city, which are written in this book.
>
> —Revelation 22:18–19

Sobering thoughts.

Prayer

Almighty, everlasting God, cause my heart to fall in love with Your Word to a greater degree than ever before. I ask for a passion to read the scriptures with a heart tender toward learning Your sacred truths. Help me to live by its standard of holiness and purity. I vow to uphold it with all my heart. Amen.

◆ eleven ◆

FALSE SHEPHERDS

How far, how deep, how wide does true love go? What lengths is a human heart willing to go to prove undying, unselfish love? When you look at a person, there is no human way to know what's inside of them. But God knows! He knows who the true shepherds are. He knows which ones are leading the flocks down the paths of righteousness.

The clothing designer knows his or her clothing very well, for they created them. The carpenter in the woodshop knows his workmanship very well, for he created and designed the pieces. How much more the Most High God, the great I AM, who knows His little beings very well, having made them and *knowing* them before they were placed into the capsule of time?

> Before I formed you in the womb I knew you.
>
> —Jeremiah 1:5

It is a wonderful thing to understand that you were known before you ever came into being! Every human heart desires someone in their life who can "know" them just as they are.

There is also an innate desire to know love in ever deepening ways. Since God *is* Love, this is His best business! Ongoing, increasing love is a way of life for those held in the arms of God the Father. He has loved the whole world before its foundation and has sent His Son Jesus to perpetuate and manifest loving truth into every part of our being. No one has to wallow in their predicaments, sorrows, pains, bondages, or sins. The Holy Carpenter from Galilee became the divine hope chest for His holy bride, who is in covenant with Him to be without spot or wrinkle (Eph. 5:27). How interesting that John the beloved leaned upon the chest of Jesus. He knew Jesus was His only hope! (John 13:23–25).

The deceiver who fell from heaven does not want us to find our destiny of love in God. This vicious deceiver perpetrates his work through lies since he is the, "Father of lies" (John 8:44). This is *his* best business! Deceit! His first recorded words in Genesis were filled with it when he questioned God's orders to Adam and Eve about not eating the fruit of one of the trees. Satan, that sly, evil serpent said, "You surely shall not die" (Gen. 3:4). Liar! Adam and Eve are dead! They died just as the Almighty Jehovah God said they would if they disobeyed. Questioning the very words of God has gone on for millennia.

THE FIGHT IS ON

The fight for truth is still on! In fact, many these days are interpreting or using the Bible to say whatever they want it to say. Just like satan in the Garden of Eden, they twist, turn, shake it, and bake it whichever way they want to justify their views. In their hands, it's a hot commodity all right, but it's one that leads to the fire of hell:

> For time will come when they will not endure sound doctrine; but wanting to have their ears tickled, they will accumulate for themselves teachers in accordance to their desires; and will turn away their ears from the truth, and will turn aside to myths.
>
> —2 Timothy 4:3–4

These teachers or shepherds have always been around, but their contaminating doctrines will increase in the Last Days.

We must realize it's extremely dangerous to read anything else into the Word of God than what it says. It's God's eternal Word. It changes not. But mankind is full of folly, selfishly wanting their own way. Many dilute it to affirm their compromised lifestyles. First Timothy 1:5–11 shows quite clearly how the Law is good, if one uses it lawfully:

> But the goal of our instruction is love from a pure heart and a good conscience and a sincere faith. For some men, straying from these things, have turned aside to fruitless discussion, wanting to be teachers of the Law, even though they do not understand either what they are saying or the matters about which they make confident assertions. But we know that the Law is good, if one uses it lawfully, realizing the fact that law is not made for a righteous man, but for those who are lawless and rebellious, for the ungodly and sinners, for the unholy and profane, for those who kill their fathers or mothers, for murderers and immoral men and homosexuals and kidnappers and liars and perjurers, and whatever else

> is contrary to sound teaching according to the glorious gospel of the blessed God, with which I have been entrusted.

How can any pastor, teacher, or minister of the gospel of our Lord possibly interpret those verses to mean anything other than what they say? The Almighty God's Word is not mincemeat. It's divine Truth, holy, powerful, and everlasting (Ps. 119). His Word existed before we did. What makes us think we can change it? Be sure of this, He is a holy God and anything that comes into His presence must be holy. There is a spiritual mark being placed on us by the Lord for those who are holy and those who are profane, according to Leviticus 10:10.

We have all sinned in various ways whether it's immorality, lying, cheating, stealing, being jealous, gossip, slander, or revenge, so we all need to be cleaned up (Rom 3:23)! Repentance through Jesus is the only gateway of cleansing and purification that leads to joyful, everlasting life (Rom. 3:24).

No one in good conscience, from a heart of love for God's truth, could ever condone or promote same-sex unions or gay marriages knowing full well it's contrary to His holy covenant. The heart of God the Father is broken over man's attempt to rework passages of divine revelation, risking eternal damnation (Rev. 22:11–19). Our loving Lord takes no pleasure in the death of sinners (Ezek. 18:32). But more people than at any other time in history are making a mockery of the redemption at Calvary with their self-interpretive, self-serving ways. Their hearts are not aligned with the Holy Spirit. The fight continues to rage for the soul of mankind! The battle for the true Bride of Christ, Armageddon, is approaching at lightning speed!

How Do You Know?

Let's go back to the opening question. What lengths is a person willing to go to prove undying, unselfish love? How much of themselves are they willing to sacrifice? When you look at a person, how do you know what's inside of them? How can you know their depth of love? How do you recognize false shepherds from the true ones? How can you keep from being deceived by other people, satan, or his cohorts? Are you aware satan can portray himself as an angel of light? He's a masterful, maligned magician (2 Cor. 11:14; Exod. 7). How are you to know truth from untruth?

Let me answer that first by taking a worldly example. The United States government, in regard to bogus bills, tells its security agents they need to know the *real* so well, they'll immediately be able to spot the false.

Spiritually speaking then, you've got to know the Bible, inside and out. You've got to know it for yourself. You've got to digest the whole book. Otherwise you'll be easily turned aside from the straight and narrow path of light and truth (Matt. 4:4).

This is why the preceding chapter of this book was written. There is coming a time soon when the Word of God will be a very hot commodity! Multitudes of people are becoming more restless as the world grows darker (Isa. 60). They'll begin searching for knowledge, truth, and revelation as never before. They will begin to devour God's Word for themselves day and night to see what He has to say about these things. It's coming. Watch and see. It will be an exciting time for the true Bride of Christ, the church.

> Now these were more noble-minded than those in Thessalonica, for they received the word with great eagerness, examining the Scriptures daily, to see whether these things were so.
>
> —Acts 17:11

Don't Be Deceived!

We must also be aware that even if one does know God's Word, one could still be deceived! You might be asking, "How could this be?" The reason is that Scripture must be digested with surrender to God and passionate love for Him! Satan himself knows the Bible very well, but there is no love in him. He's a liar and a murderer. "The demons also believe and shudder" (James 2:19). Demons shudder at the power and authority of God, but there's no surrendering to Him who is love. Shockingly, satan was brazen enough to use the scriptures in an attempt to entice Jesus to sin (Matt. 4). Let us be alert to these things.

It's far too easy to be swayed into false doctrines if you do not know for yourself what the Almighty God has spoken through His written Word, applying it with grace, truth, and love. Around the globe people are falling deeper into darkness because the spirit of deception is blinding their eyes. They may be relying too heavily upon teachers or pastors. Therefore, they are not aware satan can appear as an angel of light. His cheap disguises look good, but are deadly:

> For such men are false apostles, deceitful workers, disguising themselves as apostles of

> Christ, and no wonder, for even Satan disguises himself as an angel of light.
>
> —2 Corinthians 11:13–14

How are you going to know the difference? You must know the Word of God for yourself. You must know the Holy Spirit and He will teach you all things:

> If anyone loves Me, he will keep My word; and My Father will love him, and We will come to him, and make Our abode with him. He who does not love Me does not keep My Words; and the word which you hear is not Mine, but the Father's who sent Me. But the Helper, the Holy Spirit, whom the Father will send in My name, He will teach you all things, and bring to your remembrance all that I said to you.
>
> —John 14:23–24, 26

Again, we must be alert and cautious. You must get to know the Lord personally. There has begun to be an alarming amount of people, including shepherds of the flocks of many denominations, who piecemeal the Word of God, never really delving into its entirety, "Man shall not live on bread alone, but on every word that proceeds out of the mouth of God" (Matt. 4:4). One must take in the whole Bible, not just bits and pieces here and there. Likewise, many snack on it with the excuse of time constraints. Nevertheless, they don't have a problem with time constraints when sitting down to a big dinner in a restaurant lingering for several hours. The Word of God is spiritual sustenance, and if it were taken in as the feast it is, life abundant would flow. "Behold, I stand at the door and knock; if anyone hears My voice and opens the door, I will come in to him and will dine with him and he with Me" (Rev. 3:20). If you want dinner reservations with the King of kings, then call on Him! What a glorious feast!

WHAT'S THE STANDARD?

How many sermons have you heard in your lifetime? How many Sunday mornings, how many Sunday School classes, how many conferences have you been to and you still have not encountered the living Lord of life in a personal way that you would know victory in your life over sin, flesh, and the devil?

> You search the scriptures because you think that in them you have eternal life; and it is these that bear witness of Me; and you are unwilling to come to Me, that you may have life.
>
> —John 5:39

Many of the shepherds of the flocks teach Sunday after Sunday about being good and doing good. That's fine. Anyone can probably do that. However, it's not going to get people deep enough in the scriptures where they can take flight in revelation, knowledge, and fear of the Lord (Isa. 11). Let the people pick up their Bibles and carry them to church! If not there, where?

How are you going to discern the true man or woman of God? I don't want to burst anyone's bubble, but it's sure not going to be how well they clean up, how much charisma they have, what a good teacher or preacher they are, how well they've memorized scriptures, how many community things they're involved in, or how many miracles they've been a part of. None of these things, although good, are not the standard. Matthew 7:20–21 is the key:

> So then, you will know them by their fruits. Not everyone who says to Me, 'Lord, Lord,' will enter the kingdom of heaven; but he who does the will of My Father who is in heaven. Many will say to Me on that day, 'Lord, did we not prophesy in Your name, and in Your name cast out demons, and in Your name perform many miracles?' And then I will declare to them, 'I never knew you; depart from Me, you who practice lawlessness.'

In this passage of Matthew we see spectacular things being done in Jesus' name, but they do not know the Savior intimately. Could they be in it for show and tell? Are they looking for name and fame? The world has its "do-gooders" and we are thankful for all they do. But without a commitment of the pure, ordained love of God, they risk losing their eternal reward.

To Know Him Is to Love Him!

Our Lord says to those with impure hearts and motives, "I never knew you; depart from Me, you who practice lawlessness." (See Matthew 7:23.) Harsh? Not really. It has never been about "doing," it's about "being" in fellowship and communion with the Lord. The Savior always honors His Name, but "carriers" of the Good News may end up in hell like Judas Iscariot if they're not careful! What is the depth of their love? To *know* Him is to love Him as an old song used to say. You'll know them by their fruits, and the first fruit of the Holy Spirit is love.

Godly love is pure, holy, and sacrificial. A good and godly shepherd will live the words of John 12:24–25:

> Truly, truly, I say to you, unless a grain of wheat falls into the earth and dies, it remains by itself alone; but if it dies it bears much fruit. He who loves his life loses it; and he who hates his life in this world shall keep it to life eternal.

Many think this walk with God is about good deeds. It is, but it's not. In other words, you may travel the world over, evangelize thousands, you may do mighty signs and wonders, but could still lose your own soul. This should not shock you if you know the Word of God. In Acts 19 there were seven sons of Sceva who were attempting to use the name of Jesus. Unfortunately, this kind of use and abuse goes on far too often under the guise of Christianity. But these men were horrified when the demon jumped on them, overpowering them as they fled naked and wounded! They did not know such a thing could happen! The devil speaks audibly to these sons of Sceva saying, "I recognize Jesus, and know about Paul, but who are you?" (Acts 19:13–17). Who are you?

The devil knows who you are. He knows if you belong to God or not. And of course, God knows who you are! He knows if you know Him by head or by heart. God will not allow anyone to get by with using and abusing His Word, at least, not for very long. If this kind of thing could happen to the sons of Sceva, it can happen now and indeed has for generations. Scripture tells us that demons are indeed subject to those who are in Christ, but that we ought to rejoice more in the fact that our names are written in heaven (Luke

9:17–20)! Some ministries have their own agendas and do not align with the truth of God's Word. The gay marriage issue is a prime example of this. There will be accountability!

Jesus speaks some alarming words to Philip in John 14:9: "Have I been so long with you, and yet, you have not come to know Me, Philip?" It's not so much about head knowledge as it is heart knowledge. Certainly we must know the Word of God, but more so to know Him! Do you know Him personally, heart to heart? The bloody birthing of eternal salvation at Calvary bought our access behind the veil, and the invitation wasn't just for the high priest any longer. It was now open for all who would enter into that intimate place with God (Luke 23:45; Heb. 9). Have you entered in? If not, why not?

Who's Leading?

We need to get real with Jesus. We've simply got to get to know Him for ourselves. We need to know the perfect pitch of the sound of His perfect voice so that another we will not follow. Much of the Gospel in John 10 is devoted to the Good Shepherd and gives an example of how good shepherds lead. They certainly aren't bent on pleasing themselves or their fleshy desires. It's getting harder to find good shepherds who follow in the Lord's footsteps, willing to lay down glamour, glitter, and gold for the kingdom of God. Those who do are as shining jewels in the land willing to lay their lives down for their flock.

> And the Lord their God will save them in that day as the flock of His people; for they are as the stones of a crown, sparkling in His land.
>
> —Zechariah 9:16

Unfortunately, false ones have crept in among us, distorting the Word of God. They seem to value the acceptance of men more than God, vying instead to be popular or politically correct. They would do well to check in with Paul in Galatians 1:10, "For am I now seeking the favor of men, or of God? Or am I striving to please men? If I were still trying to please men, I would not be a bond-servant of Christ." Being a bondservant of the Lord Jesus is where we all should be, not just the pastors and teachers. One must be sold-out to Him no matter what the cost. But cost is an ill-forgotten word in most Christian cultures of today. Sadly, it shows. We've traded the pleasures of God's presence and power for the pleasures of an ease-ridden society. No one wants to rock any boats anymore, much less get out and walk on water!

A powerful biblical example of compromise is in Exodus 32:25 where Moses' brother Aaron allows the people to get out of control, going so far as to make a golden calf and calling it the god who brought them out of Egypt! Aaron! Of all people! Think of all the signs, wonders, and miracles he had seen, and yet he chose to please the crowd rather than please God. Many people died as a result of his sin! In the following chapter the Lord told Moses that they could go ahead and go to the Promised Land, even promising to send an angel in front of them, but that He Himself would not go with them. Angels are nice, but there's nothing like the Lord's presence! But Moses pleaded with God that if His presence did not go with them, they would not go! Are our pastors crying out to God in this manner?

An Accounting

The prophet Isaiah gives an admonition in 56:11 about shepherds who have no understanding and who have all turned to their own way. We see this all too often in the media. Even in my hometown, the newspaper carried a glowing article with several pictures of a pastor who married his male partner. Many attended this "wedding." Our society has become so de-sensitized to anything pure and holy that many people simply are not fazed by the unrighteousness of this act to any degree whatsoever. But I hear the Lord's heart crying for them! He loves them and wants them in His house! He wants His bride, the church, to be under His holy, divinely designed covenant, not the world's version of it.

In many so-called Christian arenas, no longer is the banner of God's holy love held in high esteem as the church itself ordains gay and lesbian pastors, "They fear the Lord and served their own gods according to the custom of the nations from among whom they had been carried away into exile" (2 Kings 17:33, 41). A mixture of gods does not work! This is what the Israelites did when they came out of Egypt and wandered for forty years. This unholy mixing of God's Word still causes wanderings that lead to death.

Are we reading the same Bible?

There will be an eternal accounting of these things. The true body of believers will sense a deep grieving within their souls for the contamination and abominations that have crept into the church. Who is going to cry out upon the altars? Jeremiah, known as the weeping prophet, had much to say about false shepherds. Writing under the unction of the Holy Spirit, he said:

> Many shepherds have ruined My vineyard, they have trampled down My field; they have made My pleasant field a desolate wilderness. It has been made a desolation, desolate, it mourns before Me; the whole land has been made desolate, because no man lays it to heart.
>
> —Jeremiah 12:10

These are shocking words! Let us understand this sharp admonition is directed at God's own people, not the world. We ought to know better. We must read these things for ourselves.

Line of Distinction Marred

The shepherds in the churches are called to lead their flocks in righteousness and in the truth of holy Scripture. But far too often the line of distinction between the church and the world is marred. Of course there are many good pastors and leaders who are endowed with grace, humility, love, purity, and holiness, upholding God's truths as ordained in the Bible. Thank God for them! I am referring only to those who choose to compromise the Word of God. Let us take heed to the burning words used to begin chapter 23 of Jeremiah: "Woe to the shepherds who are destroying and scattering the sheep of My pasture!"

This Old Testament prophet continues his lament concerning false shepherds throughout chapter 25. Verse 33 is rather poignant:

> Wail, you shepherds, and cry; and wallow in ashes, you masters of the flock; for the days of your dispersions have come, and you shall fall like a choice vessel…the Lord is destroying their pasture.

What do these things mean other than many of the shepherds are not aligning themselves with the infallible Word of God? Studying Jeremiah, you know his heartache in seeing leaders go astray. Shockingly, as if he can't say it strong enough, he repeats his dismay in 50:6, "My people have become lost sheep; their shepherds have led them astray."

In John 10, Jesus shows us the barometer of a true pastor or leader. They're the ones who will not follow any voice than that of the true Shepherd, Jesus Christ. They are willing to lay down their lives for Him! We need true shepherds once again who are willing to guard their sheep with their very lives. Where are they?

How many are reading the Bible? And if they are, how could they take it upon themselves either to ignore sacred truths or redistribute the wording to fit their sinful lifestyles? The cost of ignorance is very high. Last Days deceptions are running rampant in this hour. Spiritual weapons of mass destruction by satan are becoming more blatant than ever before, and one of his greatest ones is diluting the scriptures. Let us awake from our sickly slumber and call out to God for mercy!

I want you to know that deception is seeping in to such a degree that it is taking people into hell quicker than anything else! The end will come. It's inevitable. The Armageddon bridal battle is nearing. Will we be ready? Will we be saved?

When the Lord comes again, He asks if there will be faith on the earth (Luke 18:8). What a question! Why would He ask that? I believe it's because many will have distorted, defiled, and compromised the pure, holy Gospel of Jesus Christ to the point that true faith in Him will be hard to find!

A Quick Reality

When one looks into Acts 5, we see the dialogue between Peter and a married couple who attempted to deceive the church, saying they were in fact giving the entire amount of the sale of their property to the Lord. But Peter, being the discerning shepherd of the flock that he was, quickly brought Ananias and Sapphira into accountability. When confronted, they still lied and denied the amount of their offering. Each one died instantly! This was a quick and sure judgment by our righteous God. Harsh? Maybe. But probably not. They knew the Ten Commandments. They knew the One that said, "Thou shalt not lie."

> Behold then the kindness and severity of God.
>
> —Romans 11:22

So whether immediate, or in days to come, no one can break God's laws for long and get by with it. He is holy and eternal, and there is no unrighteousness in Him. Therefore anything that comes near Him will be judged holy or unholy, either of which determines life or death eternal. Why gamble with that? Do we really want to question and argue with such an Almighty God who formed heaven and earth with just a blast of His nostrils? (Ps. 18:15). What power is this that mankind can toy with it? Who among us is so brash as to be unwilling to bend or bow to His divine decrees? Sadly, too many. However, while one has breath in his chest, one can repent of such insolence and pride. Can we take this moment right now and do that while it is still called today (Heb. 4:7)?

Finally, take a good look at Ezekiel. He takes up a whole chapter (34) to speak to false shepherds who haven't been giving their congregations good, wholesome, biblical truth, and their people are dying on the vine. These same reverends have stopped looking for the lost, sick, and dying, because they have become corrupt. They're busy feeding themselves comfort, ease, and prominence so they'll be accepted in influential social circles. They give the people what they want to hear, not what they ought to hear.

It's getting harder to find a message in pulpits these days that calls sin, sin. Is it any wonder when some pastors may be caught up in diverse sins of greed, adultery, fornication, homosexuality, pride, spousal abuse, thievery, or jealousy? Too often the world's menu is offered, defining sinful behaviors in the context of scientific reasoning, rather than what it really is—sin. The gay lifestyle is one of those sins. And sin needs to be repented of, pure and simple. The flock should be looking to feed themselves, going past the infancy of their spiritual rebirth (Heb. 5:11–14). We're admonished in Hebrews 5:14, "But solid food is for the mature, who because of practice have their senses trained to discern good and evil."

The prophet Ezekiel tells us the Lord is also judging the sheep (Ezek. 34). Those who expect to be bottle-fed each week by their pastor are in for a powerless lifestyle. Watered-down, diluted teachings are filtered with excuses. The Lord declares in Ezekiel 34:8:

> Therefore, you shepherds, hear the word of the Lord: 'As I live,' declares the Lord, 'surely because My flock has become a prey, My flock has even become food for all the beasts of the field for lack of a shepherd, and My shepherds did not search for My flock, but rather the shepherds fed themselves and did not feed My flock.'

But there is hope for all of us, shepherds and sheep alike, no matter what we've done! Jesus has a heart of compassion and love for all who have gone astray: "And seeing the multitudes, He felt compassion on them, because they were distressed and downcast like sheep without a shepherd" (Matt. 9:36). Can we say in all honesty, the Lord is my Shepherd, I shall not want (Ps. 23)? O what a wonderful Savior we have!

Stop being spoonfed by others. Love them. Love people. But look into the Word of God for yourself. Digest it. Begin to soak it in. Grow up! It's time to know the divine Shepherd for yourself! He is truth, and the truth shall set you free (John 8:32)!

Prayer

O divine Savior, I confess my need to know You for myself. Let me not be led astray by the shifting ways of man, but let me stand on the solid ground of Your Holy Word. My heart delights to know Your written Word so that purity and the joy of living will encompass me all the days of my life. Amen.

◆ twelve ◆

INTIMACY WITH GOD

LET'S BEGIN WITH what it is not.

Not too long ago, our ministry received two identical letters, one week apart, from some anonymous *pastor* in California, or, so he stated. It immediately became apparent why he did not sign his name. The two paged, single-spaced typed letter was filled with grotesque, pornographic, homosexual language of his delusional encounters with Jesus. The letter was so graphically disgusting that we didn't even want it in our garbage bin! It appeared to be some kind of a form letter and was perhaps sent out to others as well. It alluded to wanting answers for these so-called explicit, intimate encounters with the Lord Jesus.

Obviously, this is *not* what intimacy with God is! God is spirit. He is holy and commands us to be holy as He is holy.

> For I am the Lord your God. Consecrate yourselves therefore, and be holy; for I am holy. And you shall not make yourselves unclean with any of the swarming things that swarm the earth. For I am the Lord, who brought you up from the land of Egypt, to be your God; thus you shall be holy for I am holy.
>
> —Leviticus 11:44–45

In the Book of Leviticus 10:10 and 11:47, God again instructs His people to make themselves a distinction so the unclean can be clearly seen from the unclean. Indeed the Word, Jesus, became flesh and dwelt among us, but God's Word is pure, holy, and truth. (John 1:14). The Gospel of John says in 3:6, "That which is born of the flesh is flesh, and that which is born of the Spirit is spirit." True born-again believers in the Savior Jesus Christ know this!

Accountability

As stated in the last chapter, if this man who wrote this aforementioned letter is indeed a pastor, if he shepherds a flock, then we must grieve the signs of the times we are in! It's a sign of the end! (Matt. 24–25). That end will indeed come because God's Word has decreed it. The last revelation of God tells us that when the doors are closed on time and eternity begins, "Nothing unclean and no one who practices abomination and lying shall ever come into it [heaven]...Outside are the dogs and the sorcerers, and the immoral persons..." (Rev. 21:27; 22:15). Those in leadership in the body of Christ will be held accountable just like everyone else, but even more so because they're the ones leading their flocks to either life or death. Sadly, while some of them preach a form of freedom, "They themselves are slaves of corruption" giving approval for homosexuality and other unclean things" (2 Pet. 2:19).

The most intimate book in the Bible, Song of Songs (or Song of Solomon), was written as a beautiful, poetic, allegorical theme for the Second Coming of Christ for His beautiful bride, the church. Note that it is a love relationship between a bride and a bridegroom, a man and a woman. It's not about two men or two women. When the Word made flesh, Jesus, comes to this earth again, it will be to take His bride away to be with Him forever. Nowhere does Scripture tell us He is coming for a bridegroom! One cannot, in all truth, dare to believe otherwise. One cannot, in all truth, believe the Almighty, holy God would sanction any other kind of marriage than that between a man and a woman. It's especially clear in this particular book of the Bible. In a physical marriage of a man and wife, the two bodies have been perfectly designed to fit together for procreation. Likewise spiritually, Christ is the Head and His body is the church work together to produce spiritual children for the kingdom of God. Again, remember, "Flesh gives birth to flesh, spirit gives birth to spirit" (John 3:6). It's a holy union. It's a beautiful marriage! There is great joy!

Kisses

We can see in the opening of Song of Songs, verse two, a rather intimate statement: "May He kiss me with the kisses of His mouth." This is holy! This is very holy! And what an amazingly powerful thing it is! This speaks of the Word of God and the Holy Spirit going into our very being and touching our minds and hearts, bringing transformation! One must realize how perfectly this fits in with Deuteronomy 30:14, "But the Word is very near you, in your mouth and in your heart, that you may observe it." (See also Romans 10:8.) One of the meanings in Greek is that mouth to mouth is a direct communication as in eye to eye.[1] You can liken it to those times when you've really wanted to make a point in talking to someone, perhaps your child, and you get right up to their face so they can feel your breath as you look them straight in the eye and say, "Listen to me!" That's direct, personal communication! This is what we want from God isn't it? We want to know Him up close for ourselves so we can love and obey Him. We don't want religion because it is tiring and unproductive—what we want is *relationship*!

Likewise that verse speaks volumes on the way the rest of the book proceeds through this allegorical relationship between the church and our heavenly Bridegroom, Jesus Christ. It broadly displays the intimacy with God that we are to pursue. It's every man, woman, and child for himself. No one can give this relationship to you. You must seek for it yourself. Know Jesus for yourself, not through others.

One might also see that in a mouth-to-mouth situation, this can be likened to needing resuscitation. Many times we've either seen on TV, or experienced it in some way ourselves, someone using mouth-to-mouth resuscitation to try to save a life.

In Ezekiel 37 the Lord directs the prophet to speak breath and life into dry bones! Many people have dry, brittle lives. No hope. No future. No life. They need resuscitation! They need the breath of God to enter into them. They need healing life in their body, mind, heart, and soul. They need the kiss of God! They need to press into Him with all their being and seek His face while He may be found and while they have earthly breath in them. Do you know someone who needs this? Could it be you? Do you want to breathe fresh, vibrant air? Do you want to live life abundantly, full and holy?

We need to open our mouth so God can fill us. The Lord wants us to be like a baby bird waiting to be fed.

The Lord tells us Psalm 81:10, "I, the Lord, am your God, who brought you up from the land of Egypt; open your mouth wide and I will fill it." And don't you know, little birds are always hungry, chirping loudly, wanting more and more so they can get strong and fly into the heights of heaven? That's where we want to go as well! God's breath declares in Psalm 34:8, "Taste and see that I am good." If we need knowledge of God, if we need purpose in our lives, if we need a friend that sticks closer than a brother, if we need all the riches of our inheritance in Christ, then we need to open up our mouths and let God fill it. We need to know this kind of intimacy with Him through His written Word. We must know Him by heart!

Purity

Satan will always try to distort this divine and holy love relationship the Lord has with His followers. Certainly evil comes to do nothing but rob, kill, and destroy (John 10:10). But we are called to come to God with deep reverence and to rejoice before Him with much trembling, awe, and holy fear. This cannot be more clearly stated than what it says in Psalm 2:10–12, which invites us to the Son, with some ancient versions rendering, "Do homage purely."[2] The only distortion in an intimate relationship with God comes from His foes. The world cannot know of this holy union and therefore does all it can to diminish it. Not surprising. They are the ones trying to redefine marriage. They know nothing of the *purity* of the Bride of Christ. They are untaught and unstable, distorting scriptures to their own destruction, as well as those who call themselves Christians not discerning the body of

Christ (2 Pet. 3:16; 1 Cor. 11:27–30). The Lord Jesus is not going to blaze the eastern skies with His Second Coming by looking for a compromised, contaminated Bride! His eyes will be aflame with passion for the one clothed in white garments, which are the righteous acts of the saints (Rev. 19:8).

Deep Calls to Deep

It is a fact that every human has an ingrained need to be loved. Psalm 42:7 says that "Deep calls to deep," and so it is that the deepest part of us cries out to our Creator God to know Him deeply. Many of you know as you met the love of your life, superficiality just wouldn't do! You wanted to get to know that person as much as possible. You wanted to spend as much time with them as you could. You spent hours talking in order to get to know one another. Then the attraction began to go deeper than just mere polite conversation. It went to matters of the heart, didn't it? Then, if so ordained by God, marriage followed and the relationship went deeper still. We will examine this aspect in a later chapter. We will examine just how we really are the Bride of Christ. But for now let it be said that this is exactly what Song of Songs is all about. The allegory is beautiful for the human heart and spirit. It was given by the breath of God that we might breathe Him in to ever-deepening levels. This enables us to overcome many adverse things in life because we *know* who we belong to! We know His grace and His power that can defeat any enemy that assails us. Oh, to know Him more! What joy!

And so it is, that we do not desire to know our beloved King superficially, but as deep, wide, and as high as possible (Eph. 3:16–19). We can even be filled up with the Holy Spirit! That's what Pentecost brought. Those precious souls were filled to overflowing, and they just were not themselves! I don't know about you, but I'd just rather not be myself because I have a tendency to mess up everything! I'd rather be consumed into the holy presence of the Lord and be all He wants me to be. I'd rather go on His strength, His anointing, and His power than any of my own sinful, fleshy frailty. Those 120 people in that Upper Room could not hold back the peculiar behavior that came forth! They were changed from operating within the confines of the flesh to the power of the Holy Spirit, having been overtaken by Him. Do you want this? If you give the right answer, you will kiss the Lord according to Proverbs 24:26.

More to It

There's more to this kissing, that is spoken of in Song of Songs. As I've noted, it's inviting the breath of God, His Spirit, to enter into your very being. Let us realize that God's breath quickens our mortal bodies, bringing strength, healing, and purity of purpose. Romans 8:11 is wonderful! "But if the Spirit of Him who raised Jesus from the dead dwells in you, He who raised Christ Jesus from the dead will also give life to your mortal bodies through His Spirit who indwells you."

King David, who was a man after God's own heart, uttered a beautiful phrase in Psalm 63 when he spoke of his soul thirsting for God, but also his flesh yearned for Him as well. What does that mean? Certainly not perversion! David prayed precisely according to God's Word in Romans 8:11 before it was ever written. David longed to be entirely filled up with the holiness and purity of the Lord God Almighty—his mind, body, and soul. This is intimacy with God! This is true holiness.

Kindred Spirits

Some try to distort the deep friendship David had with Jonathan (1 Kings 18:1–4; 20; 2 Kings 1:17–27). When David says that Jonathan's love was more wonderful than the love of women, he was speaking of the closeness of a deep friendship. This is the kind of friendship where two hearts are knitted together in an understanding and sharing of the deep, spiritual things of God. Jonathan recognized the anointing on David's life; therefore, he knew David by *spirit.* And David knew Jonathan by *spirit,* knowing him to be a trustworthy friend. They were as we call it today like-minded, or kindred spirits.

I know this kind of friendship firsthand because I have a friend I love very much and I know loves me as well. We encourage and challenge each other in our walk with the Lord to a greater degree than an average friendship. We know we can count on one another to do spiritual warfare in time of great need. This was true for David and Jonathan as the scriptures attest. Jonathan protected David even unto death. "Greater love has no one than this, that one lay down his life for his friends" (John 15:13). God's Word also declares in Proverbs 17:17 that a true friend loves at all times. This in no way suggests perversion. But the ungodly would have us think otherwise, especially those who do not live in purity and holiness according to God's Word.

One must also look into Romans 1:21–28 to see these things more clearly regarding ungodly lusts of the flesh that are condemned by God. It must be quoted here in its entirety, or some may not read it at all!

> For even though they knew God, they did not honor Him as God, or give thanks; but they became futile in their speculations, and their foolish heart was darkened. Professing to be wise, they became fools, and exchanged the glory of the incorruptible God for an image in the form of corruptible man and of birds and four-footed animals and crawling creatures. Therefore God gave them over in the lusts of their hearts to impurity, that their bodies might be dishonored among them. For they exchanged the truth of God for a lie, and worshipped and served the creature rather than the Creator, who is blessed forever. Amen. For this reason God gave them over to degrading passions; for their women exchanged the natural function for that which is unnatural, and in the same way also the men abandoned the natural function of the woman and burned in their desire toward one another, men with men committing indecent acts and receiving in their own person the due penalty of their error. And just as they did not see fit to acknowledge God any longer, God gave them over to a depraved mind, to do those things which are not proper.

Water and Blood

Scripture shows us there is a friend who sticks *closer* than a brother (Prov. 18:24). Oh, that we might all have such a friend! Again, this was the relationship between King David and Jonathan. Have you ever heard the saying,

"Blood is thicker than water?" This of course, refers to a family bloodline. But it does not necessarily assure *closeness*, as many of us well know. However, it can be found through the bloodline of Jesus and the family of God! That's because blood and water flowed from the Savior's pierced side (John 19:34). We are not orphans. We will know Abba Father by the spirit of adoption (Rom. 8:23). These family ties are made of heavenly strength and last eternally!

True followers of Christ will not allow the world to distort the kind of friendship that David and Jonathan had. We're going to need these kinds of friendships as our spiritual allies. Why? Because of what's coming! The Armageddon battle that's soon to be upon us will be filled with many betrayals and traitors of true faith. Our Messiah warns of families even turning against each other (Matt. 10:21–22). So who are you going to be able to trust, other than someone you know for certain that has an intimate relationship with God? They will be trustworthy!

REPENTANCE

Intimacy with God brings a quickening to the whole man or woman. One thing about David, when he sinned, he repented. He didn't try to rationalize, criticize, blame others, make up excuses, or throw around new interpretations of God's Word. Sin is sin. It still is. It cannot be redefined and still needs to be repented of. His adultery with Bathsheba was blatant. But with a remorseful and sorrowing heart he cried out, "Create in me a clean heart, O God, and renew a steadfast spirit within me" (Ps. 52:10). Repentance for all sins against God's laws brings healing to the mind, heart, and body. Isaiah 55:3

describes great comfort: "Incline your ear and come to Me. Listen that you may live; and I will make an everlasting covenant with you, according to the faithful mercies shown to David." (See also Acts 13:34.)

Repentance is a good, clean bath in more ways than one! Could repentance heal the travesty of AIDS? Could repentance heal cancer? Could it heal our bodies? I believe it! Take into your bosom these words: "But if the Spirit of Him who raised Jesus from the dead dwells in you, He who raised Christ Jesus from the dead will also give life to your mortal bodies through His Spirit who dwells in you" (Rom. 8:11). You see, the Lord God desires that each one of us walk in fullness of life for our entire being. What a glorious revelation to know that holiness can dwell within our body as well as our spirit, as we breathe in the presence of God! That's what a heavenly kiss can do!

Prayer

Oh, Lord God, I repent of all disobedience to Your commands in holy Scripture. Like King David, I desire purity of heart. Take me into ever increasing intimacy with You that I may walk in the power of Your love. Holy Spirit, to know You is to love You. Help me to know You more! Amen.

◆ thirteen ◆

CODE OF CONDUCT

WHO'S IN CHARGE? Who's in control? You? The world? God?

The question looming larger than life these days is this: what authority is determining the code of conduct for civilized society? Where are the rules? Where are the lines being drawn? What are the perimeters? What is the standard? Who is making the decisions on what, where, when, and how "morality" or the code of conduct is to be established? By what authority are these things being determined? In other words, "Who's in charge?" Does anyone even care anymore?

The dictionary says that *morality* is described as: "a degree of conformity to moral principles; right moral conduct; particular system of morals."[1] What system of morals? What degree of moral conduct do you see around you? Many seem to be doing what is right in their own estimation or in their own eyes. They are their own authority. This is extremely dangerous ground. There can be varying degrees of self-proclaimed "morality" that can reach frightening levels. An extreme example is Hitler, who ascribed his own ideology, authority, and self-will to his own detriment along with millions of others. The world is still reeling from this demented leader.

Good News!

Human nature likes to be in charge. We all like to be in control. But a philosophy of self-described morals leaves one quite vulnerable and lonely in this vast world because you can't possibly feel covered, looked after, or protected. Here's the good news! There definitely is someone bigger than our own selves who *can* protect us! The Almighty God of all creation. And He has standards! He has drawn lines in the sands of earthly time and throughout our lives. They are set in place by a loving, heavenly Father. These standards have been set in place so we will not hurt ourselves, just as an earthly father would tell his children, "Do not cross this line into the street of oncoming traffic or you'll get hurt or even killed." But many are hurt from crossing over in disobedience to God's laws and His love. They get clipped or run down by oncoming traffic with the enemy's spiritual weapons. Unfortunately, these dear souls can be quite oblivious to severe harm in the spiritual realm. They are left spinning and reeling in life, wondering what happened. They wonder why they feel as they do, sensing an emptiness within. They've lost their identity because they're separated from Papa, from Abba Father of creation.

What's Right?

Because many in our day have taken it upon themselves to be their own authority, their own judge and jury, they walk a very thin line of eternal destruction and death. Who's to say what is right? Who's to say what is moral? They think they're calling all the shots, but they will have to give an accounting to God Himself. The heavenly Father inspired these words in

Judges 17:6, "In those days there was no king in Israel; every man did what was right in his own eyes." The Old Testament book of Judges reflects much of today's society. It tells the story of much heartache in fighting, rape, murder, betrayals, treachery, prostitution, deceit, lies, disaster, atrocities, and more. This was the result, of course, of every man doing what was right in his own eyes rather than abiding by the rules of someone bigger than themselves—the Lord Almighty! It got them nothing but heartache and sorrow.

We must take note of the way the whole book of Judges concludes. The words, "In those days there was no king in Israel; everyone did what was right in his own eyes," is stated once again so it must be very important (Judges 21:25). People wanted their own kingdom rather than that of God who is all authority, dominion, sovereignty, and kingship. What do we want? How are we doing?

Judgment follows those who do not abide by the law of the land, or in this case, by the boundaries set in place the kingdom of God, His rule, His authority. And He is the final authority! There is nothing higher, no greater degree of morality than that of our eternal God. He is the judge and jury. He is also the Savior or the Executioner, whichever way you want to go! Your way or His way!

> Seek the Lord while He may be found; call upon Him while He is near. Let the wicked forsake his way, and the unrighteous man his thoughts; and let him return to the Lord and He will have compassion on him: and to our God, for He will abundantly pardon. 'For My thoughts are not your thoughts, neither are

> your ways My ways,' declares the Lord. 'For as the heavens are higher than the earth, so are My ways higher than your ways, and My thoughts than your thoughts.'
>
> —Isaiah 55:6–9

Wouldn't today, even right now, be a good time to say to God, "I'm sorry for wanting my own desires. I'm exhausted with my self-willed ways. I know I am merely human with fleeting breath. You are divine and eternal. I want to live Your way, fulfilling Your divine code of conduct. I want to live with You forevermore!"

Chance

When we get up in the morning, we never really know for sure if we will have life and breath by the end of the day. No one knows when that final, momentous hour will come and it's all over. If a person has chosen what is right in his or her own eyes, the final destination for eternity will not be a favorable one. The scariest issue on earth dangles before those who do not know a Savior, because hour by hour, as they draw each breath closer to that final destiny, they're gambling with their eternal future. They're playing the lottery of life! It's a chance more than human thoughts or words can tally. The Almighty declares to human beings in Deuteronomy 30:15, "See, I have set before you today life and prosperity, and death and adversity." Too many are caught in a web of destruction because the world sells them a bill of goods that says, "Whatever feels good, do it," and they buy it. Why not go the *high* way, God's way, and choose life? This highway of holiness is pure and, "The unclean will not travel on it" (Isa. 35:8).

For the Christian, this is actually a fun road! It's full of vibrant life of health and happiness that can't be found anywhere else.

Deceit

Doing what is right in one's own eyes is deathly deceit, but many forge onward in their own fleshy desires completely oblivious to that fact. Sadly, the world chimes in, even cheering on the deathly pursuits. The lines of morality are blurred far beyond what anyone could have ever imagined even a generation ago. Blatant sexual images are now displayed unashamedly on radio, TV, movies, and printed ads in newspapers and magazines. It's not even so much about defining marriage anymore as it is just right out there, in your face, take it or leave it. Socially and politically, the price is going higher! Persecution will take on a new depth of drama unlike anything seen on earth. People who do not know the Savior will begin to bring harsh revenge against those who take Him at His Word, living pure and holy lives.

Death-Defying Feats

The issue is morality, plain and simple. It's not just about gay marriages, but about those who want to do what they want, in any *manner* they want. Who's to question a man and wife, when the man says he loves his wife, but needs his time out with gay men and she "understands," therefore letting him do what's right in his own eyes? "Right in his own eyes" is from Judges 17:6 and 21:25 as stated earlier.[2] Who is to question another married man and wife, the husband being a cross-dresser, and the two of them go out shopping for women's clothes so they can go on romantic dinners together dressed as two women? Who's to question whether this is normal or not, or the morality of it? Who's to question when the cross-dresser decides he's always wanted to wear a wedding gown, so he and his wife get married all over again, inviting many relatives and friends to the ceremony as they both go down the aisle of a church as brides? Ironically, everyone on the invitation list graciously accepts and joins the gala event and the whole tirade! Who is to question when a man has been married for twenty-five years and tells his wife he wants to be a woman and then after his sex-change operation they still live together as a couple? My friends, these are real-life stories for all the world to see.

Who's to question when a lesbian couple gets married in Canada and city hall is flying the gay pride flag beside the Canadian maple leaf? To speak the name of Jesus would mean greater reproach to these people. Who is to question a schoolteacher who has sex with a middle school-aged boy? These things are bizarre and complicated. But they *are* documented and have been seen openly everywhere, confusing a young and impressionable generation, not to mention even the elderly!

Isn't it interesting that people think they can play around with God's laws but when they do that with man's laws, they know full well the consequences if they break those laws? Even then, some still don't care. They'll chance it to see whether or not they'll get caught. It's the same with God's laws. Many choose to ignore them and have it their own way. But they will indeed suffer the consequences unless there is repentance.

Mortality

This new morality is really mortality. It's a death sentence. Spiritual blindness is sweeping the earth. It's the blind leading the blind, and all are heading for the precipice! One must ask, "How far will it go? Are there any limits? Are there any hindrances to going as far as anyone sees fit in their own eyes?" Trouble is brewing on the horizon!

Where is the church? Where are the saints of God? Where are the righteous ones who live by faith in God? Why are so many afraid to speak up? Where are the heroes of the faith? Where are those who are willing to die for what they believe? There are many worldly, deceived people who will die for their beliefs. But I hear the spirit of the Lord saying, "Where are My people?"

Are There Even Ten Righteous?

One must look at the great cries of intercession by Abraham before God destroyed Sodom and Gomorrah. Abraham asks God in Genesis 18, "Suppose there are fifty righteous within the city; wilt Thou indeed sweep it away and not spare the place for the sake of the fifty righteous who are in it?" (v. 24). He goes on to ask the Lord if He would take out the righteous with the unrighteous and wouldn't that be unjust? (Rom. 9:14; 11:22). The Lord tells him He would not destroy the city if fifty righteous people were found. Abraham knew Sodom and Gomorrah were rampant with sexual sins of all kinds and knew that fifty might be too big a number to ask for! He then asks the Lord if He'd still spare the city if forty-five righteous people were found. Yes. God says He would spare the entire city if only forty-five were found. For it is not His desire to destroy the righteous with the wicked. Poor Abraham; he sees destruction coming and so he bargains with the Lord, asking sheepishly if He would still spare the city if forty righteous people were found.

The scenario goes on to thirty-five, then to thirty, twenty, then finally to ten. But sadly, not even ten good, upright, pure people could be found in that entire city. Abraham's nephew, Lot, along with his wife and two daughters were led out of the city by angels because God was releasing other angels to bring fire and brimstone to destroy this sin-sick city.

Unfortunately, Lot's wife turned for a brief moment to gaze upon all she had left behind and immediately turned into a pillar of salt! Could this be you? Could you have left the death-lifestyle of drugs, alcohol, sex, gambling, lies, deceit, and other sins you were in, but have briefly checked it out again? This could be a very costly mistake. One glance is all the enemy needs to entice us back into our old fleshy ways. Once set free, stay free. It was for freedom that Jesus set us free (Gal. 5:1)!

The moral of the story is the morale of the city. There simply wasn't any morality in the city. Everyone was doing what they wanted. They were their own authority. They simply were not willing to bow their knees to a holy God who is exacting and commanding for holiness in every level of life. There were precious few in a whole city who could be saved because of their purity. What about your city? What about you?

New Man-Made Rules

This covert attack upon the soul is coming against many unsuspecting people. It's very subtle. An example is a Hollywood entertainment figure who is doing amazing humanitarian work in foreign countries. No one takes into account this movie star has stolen another woman's husband, has his baby out of wedlock, but is almost labeled a Mother Teresa of our times. There is something wrong with this picture! The acceptance of having babies out of wedlock and living together is now commonplace. Friends of God, realize this truth: even when these live-in couples do get married, they haven't "made it right" in the eyes of God. They are still living in sin. Why? Because there needs to be repentance for the sin of fornication. Without confession of sins, no one can enter into eternal life with Christ Jesus. "Or do you not know that the unrighteous shall not inherit the kingdom of God? Do not be deceived; neither fornicators, nor idolaters, nor effeminate, nor homosexuals, nor thieves, nor the covetous, nor drunkards, nor revilers, nor swindlers, shall inherit the kingdom of God" (1 Cor. 6:9–10).

Could the day come when marriage itself will be outdated or even abolished by civil authorities? This would not be fiction. "But the Spirit explicitly says that in later times some will fall away from the faith, paying attention to deceitful spirits and doctrines of demons, by means of the hypocrisy of liars seared in their own conscience as with a branding iron, men who forbid marriage" (1 Tim. 4:1–3).

This is what *Armageddon Bride* is about! A battle will ensue between the true Bride of Christ, His pure church, and those who believe otherwise. The worldly distortion of the definition of the bride and bridegroom will come into judgment. The Bible says in Psalm 34:21 that those who hate the righteous will be condemned. But those who come into the code of conduct established by our righteous God will be saved through our Bridegroom Jesus' blood that was shed at Calvary.

People all over the earth will have to decide to give their allegiance to a holy God who set up the world's first kingdom couple in Adam and Eve—or if not, spend eternity in hell separated from Him. That's the reality!

Mocking Church Services

Man's self-willed code of conduct is going to be called into account. And soon! Humanity's final hour is fast approaching. Signs of it are increasing everywhere. When the best picture nominees today for an Academy Award includes a picture about two homosexuals (*Brokeback Mountain*), and one about a father who is surgically changed from a male to a female (*Transamerica*), we had better begin to read the signposts. When gay pride organizers include a praise and worship service as part of their celebrations, the church needs a wake-up call! The church needs to be on high red alert for the power of the red blood of the Lamb of God who was slain for sinners. The church needs a major revival of repentance! These souls do not worship in "Spirit and in Truth" (John 4:23–24). We must live according to Romans 12:1:

> I urge you therefore, brethren, by the mercies of God, to present your bodies a living and holy sacrifice, acceptable to God, which is your

> spiritual service of worship. And do not be conformed to this world, but be transformed by the renewing of your mind, that you may prove what the will of God is, that which is good and acceptable and perfect.

The Lord's laws are perfect and wonderful (Ps. 119). When you're in complete submission to Him, there's peace of mind and soul. It's very comforting. You know you're covered and protected now and forevermore!

We've been forewarned of these kinds of mocking "church services" in the Last Days where man's ways are held in higher esteem than that of God. Alarmingly, we're now living them! Jesus warns, "You hypocrites, rightly did Isaiah prophesy of you, saying, 'This people honors Me with their lips, but their heart is far away from Me. But in vain do they worship Me, teaching as doctrines the precepts of men'" (Matt. 15:7–9).

This epic battle for the righteous code of conduct ordained by God the Father will be upon us in the not too distant future. Are you secure in knowing who you are and who_you belong to and that your actions have been by His decrees and ordinances? Our heavenly Bridegroom, Jesus, is coming again to take His pure, spotless bride to the celebratory eternal banquet: "Blessed are those who are invited to the marriage supper of the Lamb" (Rev. 19:9). Woe to those who choose their own way and risk eternal darkness. Choose Jesus! Our King of glory is the way out of the mess! Open the book and read the Father's Love Letters to humanity in the Bible. Every chapter says, "I love you! I love you! I am your Light. I am Your Shepherd. I am Your comforter. I am your joy. I am your song. I am your deliverer, healer, and provider. I am your friend, Savior, and Beloved. I love you! I love you!"

Our response is, "For Thy lovingkindness is before my eyes, and I have walked in Thy truth" (Ps. 26:3).

Prayer

O Lord, I worship You in Spirit and in truth according to Your holy Word. I know You are the moral standard for all humanity. Thank You for showing me the way of righteousness through Your loving grace. I surrender my heart, soul, mind, and body that I may live with You forevermore. Amen.

◆ fourteen ◆

THE ROMANCE OF ISRAEL

THE DIVINE LOVE affair for all humanity beats with a pulsating longing within the heart of our Heavenly Bridegroom, Jesus, especially for Jerusalem! The battle for His Bride will actually begin there. Why? There are a number of reasons, but one of them is simply because it's the Lord's homeland. This small nation is where His feet will touch the earth one final time at the close of all the ages. It's the only ground He walked while in the humble abode of a fleshy tent, and it's the same location of His return. The Old and New Testaments prophesy of the Lord's Second Coming, but upon His return, He will not come as He did before, a Lamb to be sacrificed for sinners. He will come as a magnificent Warrior Bridegroom roaring as the Lion of Judah and will set up a one thousand-year reign (Rev. 20).

This amazing time on earth will resemble what was originally lost to mankind in the Garden. It will showcase the Son of God in all His glory over the earth. The grand finale will emerge with every tribe, tongue and nation calling Him King of all kings! Lord of all lords! Every eye will behold Him, "every knee shall bow and every tongue confess that HE IS LORD" (Isa. 45:23; Rom. 14:11; Phil. 2:9–11). We must realize that sooner or later, every single knee has to bow, and will bow either willingly or unwillingly to the eternal King of glory, Christ Jesus, Savior of the world. *He is the Lord!* Let's be alert and not be ignorant of these things.

Precious ones, at that time there will be two options that will decide our fate: 1) did we confess with our mouth and believe the Word of God in its entirety? If so, then we shall reign with Him (Rev. 3:21). Or, 2) Did we piecemeal the scriptures by taking away, adding, diluting, or misaligning it? If so, then our part is taken away from the tree of life and the "the holy city," which is Jerusalem! The Holy Land! Israel! (See Revelation 22:19.)

DECIDE NOW

No abomination will come upon that space and place on earth. The atmosphere will be permeated with the holy domain of the beautiful, heavenly, eternal Bridegroom, Jesus! "Thus says the Lord, 'I will return to Zion and will dwell in the midst of Jerusalem. Then Jerusalem will be called the City of Truth, and the mountain of the Lord of hosts will be called the Holy Mountain" (Zech. 8:3).

Your heart decides on truth right now, today—at this moment in your life, while it is still called today because you might not have another hour, you might not have tomorrow or the next day or next year:

> For what does it profit a man to gain the whole world and forfeit his soul? For what shall a man give in exchange for his soul? For whoever is ashamed of Me and My Words in this adulterous and sinful generation, the Son of Man will also be ashamed of him when He comes in the glory of His Father with the holy angels.
>
> —Mark 8:36–38

Later may mean, "You're too late! You've missed it!" (Deut. 30:19; Heb. 3:7). The heavenly Bridegroom's heart pounds with passion because His desire is that none perish (2 Pet. 3:9).

Consider the amazing fact that truth stood right in front of Pontius Pilate, but He failed to comprehend. Truth is a Person, not a conceptual thing. Truth is Jesus Christ, the Word of God made flesh, who dwelt among us (John 18:38; John 1). As it was then, so it shall be again. But until that day, when the Lord breaks through the eastern skies for the second time, He longs for a bride without spot or wrinkle and has no desire for something that is a distortion of her (Eph. 5)!

Most Romantic

One of the most romantic things in the Bible is God's love for Israel. He tells her He is her husband! He has wooed her since the first book of Genesis when He established Abraham, Isaac, and Jacob—renamed Israel—by establishing them as a people where He could display His everlasting glory. God is sovereign and can display His glory in any way He sees fit. However, it is a scriptural fact that He loves to work through human beings, so it was only natural to find a people, a tribe, some family somewhere, that He could display His mighty, eternal works of majesty and splendor. Why this tribe? Why this group of people? We do not know for certain (Deut. 7; Rom. 9). However, what we do know beyond a shadow of a doubt is that He chose Israel. The entire Bible speaks of this. You might liken it to a phrase sometimes given when a child is born in adverse circumstances: "They didn't ask to be born." But they're born anyway. Praise the Lord! Israel didn't ask for this; it was sovereignly bestowed by God (Deut. 7:7–10).

One cannot know the mind of God. He is God and we are not, it's that simple. A finite mind cannot fathom an infinite mind. He is from everlasting to everlasting and without end. Precious friends, it's pretty silly to try to figure Him out when it is we who have the starting point and ending point! We know birth and death. He's Life Eternal. Please note as well that when the Bible calls our beloved Bridegroom Jesus the Alpha and Omega, it reflects the Word made flesh. Jesus created the time capsule along with the Father and was quite capable of intercepting that capsule whenever He desired. Time *does* have a beginning and an end, but Jesus does not. He is the Lord God Almighty. But the plan for the Lamb was set since the *foundation* of the world (John 17:24; Heb. 4:3, 9:26; Rev. 13:8–9; Matt. 13:34–36; Zech. 12).

This divine romance and the battle for the bride have always been on the heart of Jehovah God. His breath declares it so beautifully and poetically in covenantal words in Isaiah 54:5–6:

> 'For your husband is your Maker, whose name is the Lord of hosts; and your Redeemer is the Holy One of Israel, who is called the God of all the earth. For the Lord has called you, like a wife forsaken and grieved in spirit, even like a wife of one's youth when she is rejected,' says your God. 'For a brief moment I forsook you, but with great compassion I will gather you.'

He didn't say I am your wife or I am your bride. He said, I am your husband, and you are my bride. God's holy covenantal marital contract is again confirmed.

Don't Play With Fire

For those who are attempting to make the Bible as generic as possible, so that it can be a worldly, user-friendly book without stating genders and using sexless phrases, this is a stench and an abomination into the very nostrils of a holy God. Let each one beware and take heed, lest one is lost to eternal damnation by language that altars the very Word of an eternal Godhead. Playing with fire means one will get burned!

This wonderful romance that began in the Garden of Eden progresses throughout human history and will continue until the dawning of the last day of created earth as we know it. How adamantly the Lord seeks for His lovely, eternal bride:

> 'Behold, days are coming,' declares the Lord, 'when I will make a new covenant with the house of Israel and with the house of Judah, not like the covenant which I made with their fathers in the day I took them by the hand to bring them out of the land of Egypt, My covenant which they broke, although I was a husband to them,' declares the Lord.

That was Jeremiah 31:31–32. The next verse says:

> 'But this is the covenant which I will make with the house of Israel after those days,' declares the Lord, 'I will put My law within them and

> on their heart I will write it; and I will be their God, and they shall be My people.'

Israel and the church are divinely connected. We are actually one bride: "This mystery is great; but I am speaking with reference to Christ and to the church" (Eph. 5:31–32).

We're All Jewish, So Don't Become Arrogant!

The kingly Bridegroom, Jesus, is longing for His bride, which includes the church and Jewish believers in Messiah Jesus. The fact of the matter is, every Christian is Jewish on our father Abraham's side. Wonderfully, we have been grafted into the family tree:

> But if some of the branches were broken off, and you, being a wild olive, were grafted in among them and became partaker with them of the rich root of the olive tree, do not be arrogant toward the branches; but if you are arrogant, remember that it is not you who supports the root, but the root supports you. You will say then, 'Branches were broken off so that I might be grafted in.' Quite right, they were broken off for their unbelief, but you stand by your faith. Do not be conceited but fear; for if God did not spare the natural branches, neither will He spare you…and they also, if they do not continue in their unbelief, will be grafted in; for God is able to graft them in again.
>
> —Romans 11:17–21, 23

The nation of Israel is named after the legitimate son of Abraham from the beginning of the story in Genesis. It has been through his lineage that all the promises of God were given. For four thousand years the Lord used the Hebrew children to establish the kingdom of God. But for these past two thousand years, it's been mostly the Gentile believers whom He has used. But the twain shall meet soon and then shall be the beginning of the end—Armageddon (Rev. 16:16)!

The apostle Paul teaches these things in the New Testament book of Romans. Peering into chapter 2, verse 29 he tells us plainly, "But he is Jew who is one inwardly; and circumcision is that which is of the heart by the Spirit, not by the letter; and his praise is not from men, but from God." He also brings this admonition, "For I do not want you, brethren, to be uninformed of this mystery, lest you be wise in your own estimation, that a partial hardening has happened to Israel until the fullness of the Gentiles has come in, and thus all Israel will be saved" (Rom. 11:25).

The Jewish Carpenter

Jesus was a Jewish carpenter from Nazareth of Galilee. He ascended from on high to be about His father's business, and that business was to die for sinners such you and me. The Word made flesh, coming forth from God the Father, was from the womb of an earthly woman to set in place His plan for our salvation. This again shows the divine strategy of God in showcasing the family as it's meant to be: a man (Joseph) and a woman (Mary). Joseph, of course, was informed by the Holy Spirit regarding this holy, ordained family he was to be a part of. God's covenantal order for marriage was still intact! Nothing was asunder (Matt. 1:18–25).

Listen to God! Even in the birth of the Savior of the world, God the Father highlighted His divine order for the family consisting of one man and one woman. It has not changed. Man must not try to remake or redo God's laws. Anything less, causes great pain and heartache stemming from being aborted from the Father's bosom and His divine purposes for our lives.

Listen. We're *all* from the lineage of the first man and woman who birthed disobedience, dishonor, and shame through sin. We're all from the lineage of Adam and Eve that birthed contamination of God's holy covenants. So it's not surprising that the world wants to sanction "Adam and Steve"-type relationships. But it's distorted love.

Wonderfully, however, for those who choose God's ways, we can be born again into the lineage of the First Family from God's House, His pure and holy Throne Room whereby the divine designing team of Father, Son, and Holy Spirit brought forth the protocol of the family consisting of a mother and a father. How interesting then, that God should call Israel His FIRSTBORN! Children are born in the natural realm through a man and a woman. Spiritually speaking, God the Father chooses a holy bride, His people Israel, to bring forth spiritual children into the kingdom of God, "For I am a Father to Israel, and Ephraim is my firstborn" (Jer. 31:9; Ps. 89:7).

It's time to look truth straight in the eye and see what scripture has to say concerning these matters, "so that you might know the exact truth about the things you have been taught" (Luke 1:4). Who do you trust? Whom are you listening to? Do you check these things out for yourself? Or are you being blindly led like a sheep to the slaughter? The book of Hebrews expounds on Israel this way, "But you have come to Mt. Zion and to the city of the living God, the heavenly Jerusalem and to myriads of angels, and to the general assembly and church of the first born, who are enrolled in heaven, and to God, the Judge of all, and to the spirits of righteous men made perfect" (Heb. 12:21–23).

Showcase Marriages

We must remember that when it was time for the Lord to begin to align the history of man, he was adamant that Abraham's son Jacob would have a proper wife. He arranged that this man would perpetuate the dignity of God's chosen people in which to show forth His glory.

In this battle for the definition of marriage, we must take into serious account what the Almighty has to say. It's no accident that all through the scriptures, God goes to amazing lengths to showcase proper and holy marriage as ordained by Himself in the covenant between a man and a woman. Therefore, it is noteworthy to see in Genesis 28 where it is specifically written that God designed man to be connected with his counterpart, a woman. He gives explicit instructions to see that *Jacob* has the wife God selected for him from the foundations of earth.

All the patriarchs, Abraham, Isaac, and Jacob, were all joined with a woman in marriage. God didn't tell them to go out and find a good man, but a good woman! In fact, the Bible gives whole chapters to the sagas of

God choosing a rightful bride. Genesis 24 deals with choosing a wife for Isaac, who was Rebekah. Genesis 29 is about the choice of a wife for Jacob (or Israel), who was Rachel. The entire book of Ruth is about a perfect alignment of marriage between her and Boaz. The entire book of Esther once again displays another divinely orchestrated marriage between a man and a woman. Again, the entire book of Song of Songs is a holy allegory between a man and a woman, a husband and his wife, which represents the heavenly Bridegroom (Heb. 12:23).

The Bible tells this story over and over again, not the least of which are the stories of Moses and his wife, Zipporah; or the Jewish couple of Zechariah and Elizabeth, who birthed John the Baptist while stating which tribe of Israel they're from. Hosea is another prophetic look into the relationship of matrimony. Though this prophet was married to a prostituted, wayward wife, it was still less offensive than that of a homosexual affair. The stories go on and on.

Absolutely nowhere in God's Word is there a sanctioning of gay or lesbian *unions or marriages*—except as abomination. There are, however, close friendships noted in the Word of God. One I've already addressed between David and Jonathan. Some others were Ruth and Naomi (Ruth 1:14–17), Paul and Timothy (2 Tim. 1:3–4), Jesus and John (John 13:23).

Chivalry

Jesus, the Holy One of Israel, our Redeemer, did not have an earthly bride. But He does have a bride! She is a spiritual, eternal bride whom He has washed and cleansed with His own blood, and she is the embodiment of all believers in *Yeshua*, the Holy Messiah, from every tribe, tongue, and nation on earth. What an infinitely gallant and romantic thing for Him to do. He laid down His cloak of flesh and blood for her that she might cross over into eternal life and bliss with Him forever. Talk about chivalry!

The tree of Life on Calvary replaced the fallen man of the Garden of Eden. The holy, heavenly Bridegroom shed His blood in the ultimate sacrifice for His bride to purchase her eternally. The holy dowry was paid, and He wants her. He wants her! He died for her! Come all you who are thirsty and needy. Come! "Incline your ear and come to Me!" says the Lord. "Listen that you may live; and I will make an everlasting covenant with you…." (Isa. 55). Listen! Incline your ear before the end of the age, before the final curtain is drawn, before the trumpet sounds. "In that day the Branch of the Lord will be beautiful and glorious, and the fruit of the earth will be the pride and the adornment of the survivors of Israel. And it will come about that he who is left in Zion and remains in Jerusalem will be called holy—everyone who is recorded for life in Jerusalem" (Isa. 4:2–3).

Fiddler on the Roof

If you have not seen the classic movie, *Fiddler on the Roof*, you might want to view it. It shows so well how the enemy wants to destroy God's people. There's a scene where the enemy comes into a Jewish wedding to make a demonstration of his power by wreaking havoc and sorrow. It was a tearful moment to observe the devastation the authorities brought by smashing, ripping apart, and destroying everything in sight. Why choose a wedding in which to do this? Because satan desires to destroy God's holy covenant. The battle begun in the Garden of Eden has been raging for millennia. It will cause the final Armageddon Battle—for the Bride of Christ—at the close of planet earth.

But this momentous movie reflects so beautifully the love God has for His own as seen during the tender song, "Sunrise, Sunset." The young couple are standing beneath the *huppa* (canopy of marriage) with soft light glowing from a roomful of candles. Their faces reflect great joy and happiness. One becomes aware of the love and intimacy that will soon follow. Once again, as in generations past, a man and a woman have been joined in holy matrimony, repeating the cycle of life. At the sunrise of mankind there was a marriage between Adam and Eve. At the sunset of mankind, there will be a spiritual marriage between Jesus and His bride.

It's rather shocking, yet not surprising that the organization of the World Pride Festival of Gays, Lesbians, Transsexuals, and Transgenders have been trying to have their global event in the Holy City of Jerusalem. If this should happen, it will spark the beginning of the end! It can be likened to the scene in *Fiddler on the Roof* with the enemy wreaking much havoc and devastation. One must only read God's divine breath in Ezekiel 16 or Ezekiel 23 to see the outcome of these abominations. Jeremiah speaks of the pride of Judah and Jerusalem and how God will certainly destroy that pride (Jer. 13). We must all read the highest authority in the land which is the divine Word of the Most High God which says, "You shall not lie with a male as one lies with a female; it is an abomination" (Lev. 18:22). It can be no other way than God's way. Jesus didn't come to rewrite the Law, He came to fulfill it (Rom. 8).

What glorious redemption for repentant sinners! The profound prophet, Isaiah, says: "It will no longer be said to you, 'Forsaken,' nor to your land will it any longer be said, 'Desolate,' but you will be called 'My delight is in you, and to Him your land will be married. For as a young man marries a virgin, so your sons will marry you; as the bridegroom rejoices over the bride, so your God will rejoice over you" (62:4–5). Oh, the joy of a holy union! Oh, the joy of the heavenly spiritual marriage!

Israel, rejoice, your Bridegroom cometh! We will hold you dear in our prayers with great love in our hearts because you are our homeland.

Prayer

O heavenly Bridegroom Jesus, give me more revelation about Your love for Israel. I thank You for my rich inheritance in the Holy Land. May I love and defend Israel just as You do! Amen.

◆ fifteen ◆

BATTLEGROUND

TIRED, SICK, EXHAUSTED, and totally drained, I laid my head on the pillow in our hotel room in Jerusalem in December of 2003. My luggage had not arrived and I had to fall asleep in the same clothes I'd had on for three days. Nothing mattered at that moment except getting some much-needed sleep. After an hour and a half of dozing peacefully, I awoke with a jolt. I heard the voice of the Lord telling me to get up. He had something to say! When He speaks one does not count the cost to listen. Whether it is sleep deprivation, hunger, illness, imprisonment, or whatever it may be, it does not matter. When He speaks, it brings a holy reverential fear of God deep within your being and it's pure joy to obey. How much more so in the Holy Land! His timing is always perfect. We must remember that He is not on our time clock.

So I got up, knelt beside the bed, and covered my head with a blanket because I felt this was going to be a very holy encounter and I wanted to be somewhat alone. (I was sharing the room with a friend, but she had gone into the bathroom with her own encounter with God!)

I listened. Prayed. Listened some more and continued to wait. It's important to remember we ought not to rush in "where angels fear to tread." We must wait upon God and His timing, which is always perfect. Suddenly at 3:48 A.M., I began to have a very graphic vision, the details of which will be forever seared upon my mind and heart. Although I've experienced similar things before, this startled me not only because of the vivid colors and reality, but also because of its content. I could not write all of what was happening, but the Lord allowed me to transcribe just enough to alert the Body of Christ! The following is taken from my journal as the room opened up to another realm! The Lord spoke to me saying:

THE VISION

"I am stripping you down for the purpose of which I brought you here for."

Oh, God, I'm only one.

"One, among many."

I see a white horse to my right…raising up on its hind legs! I see its breath…its nostrils snorting and he's neighing! It's the Lord's horse readying for battle! He is coming soon! War! War looms everywhere and all around!

"Pray for the peoples to the ends of the earth that they might be saved!"

I shall not, I cannot, I will not, write what Thou dost not give me, My Lord! Purify my heart—perpetually, that I may only hear Thy clear, direct, and holy voice. (I kept feeling the holy fear of God upon me during this experience.)

He is saying to me, *"Joel! Joel!"* (the Old Testament book).

Yes, I know…they rush on the city…they run on the wall! Great is the army of the Lord!

My Father, my Father! The chariots and horsemen! So many horsemen encamped about Israel preparing for war! (I could see myriads of them.)

"You shall see My breath! Do not be afraid. Multitudes, multitudes in the valley of decision as the Day of Armageddon nears. Pray for them. Pray they choose ME! Pray they choose life! I am the way, the truth, and the life."

Lord, why am I here? I am only one.

"One can put a thousand demons to flight. Two can put ten thousand demons to flight (Ps. 91:7). *I am building My army. Those who will have no fear in battle shall be like My chosen who went with My servant Gideon* (Judges 7). *Only the strongest and the fittest shall be in My army. I am not a weak leader! I am the Lord God Almighty. Is anything too difficult for Me* (Jer. 32:17)? *I am coming for a bride without spot or wrinkle, and she shall be strong and healthy.*

Who shall enter My banquet table? Let him who hears stand beside Me. I am the Lord. My authority shall give you victory in your battles. My authority IS victory and it shall stand forever. My Word endures forever!"

Amen, Lord. Amen. Even so, come Lord Jesus, come!

"There is a spiritual holocaust going on! Awake! Awake! Do not slumber any longer, My people. My desire is that none perish!"

Then I saw people being herded together for judgment. Some are in churches, some are in mosques, and some are in synagogues...whole families being herded together...some in houses...some.... Then it all faded quickly and I could see no more. But it was enough! I was left shaken. Very shaken!

Revelation 19:11–14 became real to me, *"And I saw heaven opened; and behold, a white horse, and He who sat upon it is called Faithful and True; and in righteousness He judges and wages war. And His eyes are a flame of fire and upon His head are many diadems; and He has a name written upon Him which no one knows except Himself. And He is clothed with a robe dipped in blood; and His name is called The Word of God. And the armies which are in heaven, clothed in fine linen, white and clean, were following Him on white horses."*

Prophecy

Ironically, a few years later, our little two-year old grandson, who lives on the East Coast, woke up one morning exclaiming to his mommy and daddy, "Do you hear them? Do you hear them?" Since they heard nothing, they asked, "What does it sound like?" He told them he heard horses and they were running! They live in the city, so this was quite amazing. When we heard it, we all *knew* it was a "word" from the Lord and began to tremble. Joel 2:28 says, "And it will come about after this that I will pour out My Spirit on all mankind; and your sons and daughters will prophesy…"

Spiritual Holocaust

The stunning vision on that early December morning in Jerusalem was a profound prophetic revelation from the Lord. I believe it's a global wake-up call! We must heed it! The words *spiritual holocaust* kept ringing throughout my very being. Many souls are dying and going into eternal destruction. Many of them are ones we rub shoulders with every day. Do we care?

Jesus is coming again soon! Let it be known that "of that hour no one knows, not even the angels of heaven, nor the Son, but the Father alone," as it says in Matthew 24:36. But there will be telltale signs that the completion of humanity will be near, so we must read God's Word to know how to stay alert for the unfolding of these things.

One thing for sure, if your child or a friend of yours were standing in the middle of the street with a semi-truck speeding toward them, I don't think any one of us would just stand there and watch the devastation. However, this is what's happening in the spiritual realm. First Corinthians 15:46 tells us the natural proceeds the spiritual. Let us beware! Beloved, the greatest atrocity known to man—the holocaust of six million Jews in World War II—is now being mocked in cartoons in Iran! What God spoke to me in the dawn's early light of Jerusalem that day has been manifest on the playing field of real life. Even now, unbelievably, Iran has recently commissioned a contest for those who can exhibit the best cartoon depicting the "fiction of the holocaust"! The winner receives $12,000. Even the "twelve" in that amount of money speaks of carnage to the "twelve" tribes of Israel. The Armageddon battle for the true Bride of Christ is about to commence, and Israel will be a key element. We must be ready!

The darkest, most brutal, and horrendous days of mankind are about to begin. But those who know the Lord Jesus Christ will have no fear whatsoever. Isaiah 60 is upon us! This will be the church's finest hour! The battle is ensuing and those who belong to the eternal Bridegroom are more than conquerors through Him (Rom. 8:37). The final hours of humanity are written for us to study in the book of Revelation. Take note of the opening chapters and how each one concludes by admonishing those who have ears to hear what the Spirit is saying to the churches.

Do you hear the rapturous songs of heaven weaving through our days? "Holy, Holy, Holy is the Lord God Almighty, who was and who is and who is to come" (Rev. 4:8).

Listen!

You and I should chime in with Paul when he says in Romans 1:6 that he is not ashamed of the Gospel, for it is the power of God for salvation to everyone who believes, to the Jew first and then to the Gentiles. So let's march for Jesus! Luke reveals the thrust of evangelist efforts: "Thus it is written, that the Christ should suffer and rise again from the dead the third day; and that repentance for forgiveness of sins should be proclaimed in His Name to all the nations, beginning from Jerusalem" (Luke 24:46–47).

There is no other group, no other nation than Israel, whereby God has said, "I am your husband and your land shall be married to Me" (Isa. 54:5; 62:4; Jer. 31:32). God is faithful and He will protect His beautiful bride to the ends of the earth. "The Lord is a warrior" (Exod. 15:3). The chariots are circling even now!

Roses

Remember the tender Jewish couple being married in the movie, *Fiddler on the Roof*, and how moments later the enemy came in to wreak havoc? Within a matter of minutes the scene changed from this tender moment of intimate candlelight to war! This reminds me of another incident in Israel during that 2003 visit.

One day we were having a picnic in a Rose Garden overlooking Jerusalem. Nearby stood our security guard with his weapon at his side. Have you ever had a picnic like that? We have no idea in America how our brethren have to live in the Holy Land. But as I glanced down at my Bible with the sun glistening on its pages, I decided to pick one of the white roses in the garden to place within its folds. My eyes caught the soldier again and immediately I thought of "intimacy and war"...roses and war! What a picture! The intimate book of Song of Songs speaks of this connection between intimacy and war when it says, "The king has brought me into His chambers. Listen! My Beloved! Behold, He is coming, climbing on the mountains, leaping on the hills!...All of them are wielders of the sword, expert in war" (Song of Songs 1:4; 2:8; 3:8).

The Lord wants us to know our deepening spiritual intimacy with Him is equipping us for the intense battles ahead. As deep darkness begins to accelerate at an alarming pace, the glory of God will rise upon His people, His bride. At the twinkling of an eye the trumpet will sound, the skies, like a golden zipper, will rip open with a mighty roar and the Lord's glory will encompass the earth!

Tears

That first morning in Jerusalem after the dramatic vision I'd had, I was directed by the Lord to go out on the veranda and plead the Blood of Jesus over the city as the Muslim loud speakers, with their intrusiveness, called people to prayer. I was appalled at this invasion of mocking sounds. I was even more determined to call out Jesus' name, but had a hard time getting the glass door to slide open. The enemy was seemingly right in my face. I accidentally cut myself on the door trying to pry it open. Before I could find something to stop the blood from going all over the place, some of it dripped on my Bible. The passage where it fell was Joel 2:4 where it speaks of the warhorses and the noise of chariots! The clashing in the mid-heavens has already begun. I cried even more at that point knowing God had now confirmed what He had just spoken to me. This Old Testament book has been very close to my heart since a dramatic encounter I had with the Lord on August 4, 1996, when He told me to ask Him for five hundred thousand new souls for our area alone. Upon asking for scriptural confirmation, I was led to Joel 3:14 that day in 1996, "Multitudes, multitudes in the valley of decision for the day of the Lord is near in the valley of decision." Let us pray for those in that valley.

I wept much for our beloved Israel during that 2003 trip. We must begin to weep and intercede for the peace of Jerusalem as did the Lord Jesus, "And when He approached, He saw the city and wept over it, saying, 'If you had known in this day, even you, the things which make for peace! But now they have been hidden from your eyes" (Luke 19:41–42; Matt. 23:37). If it was His cry, then it's ours as well. There's a comforting promise in Psalm 122:6, "Pray for the peace of Jerusalem; may they prosper who love you."

Let's do it! Let's pray and ask the way to Zion, to the holy hill, to the Mountain of the Lord and we will be blessed on our life's journey (Jer. 50:4–5).

Holy Ground

The ground, the soil, the atmosphere, the very land of the chosen people of God in Israel, is being primed for the end-time battle. Where will our alliances be? Just as in that hotel room in the darkened, pre-dawn hours when the membrane between the natural and the spiritual realms was opened to me, it's about to burst open for all the world to see! At that precise and concise moment that has been in the bosom of the Father from all of time, He shall release His Son to get His bride and bring her home forever. Joel says at the beginning of chapter 3:

> For behold, in those days and at that time, when I restore the fortunes of Judah and Jerusalem, I will gather all the nations, and bring them down to the valley of Jehoshaphat. Then I will enter into judgment with them there on behalf of My people and My inheritance, Israel, whom they have scattered among the nations; and they have divided up My land. They have also cast lots for My people, traded a boy for a harlot, and sold a girl for wine that they may drink.

One thing is needed for you and me right now. We must know, accept, and live in the vital truth of the power of the blood of Calvary. Just as the wife of Moses, Zipporah, spoke of her husband as a bridegroom of blood, so too is our precious heavenly Bridegroom (Exod. 4:24–26)! His bride must be made pure and holy through His blood or forever be lost. It's time to circumcise our hearts and put on the righteous, holy garments of the wedding feast. Purity of purpose comes from what we're wearing physically as well as spiritually.

Proper Wedding Garments

What makes you or me think we can enter into the Bridal Feast at the end of the age if we are not clothed in God's righteousness? We must wear proper wedding clothes! In Matthew 22:1–14, the kingdom of God is likened to a king who is planning a wedding feast for his son. In this parable Jesus asks one of the guests how he got in. The man obviously had been invited but was not wearing proper wedding attire. This guest was presumptuous in thinking he could prance in without proper protocol. Jesus has him thrown out! "Many are called, but few are chosen," He said. Put on Christ! Put on the garments of salvation!

Some in the church world today are where this unfortunate man was at this banquet. They have compromised the Truth of God's Word, watering it down for itching ears so people will not have to feel "uncomfortable" in the house of God. There's no conviction of sin, which breaks the heart of Father God. These shall be thrown out into utter darkness forever. What a high price to pay for wanting our own way, our own pleasure instead of the Lord's. Our wonderful Bridegroom longs for us to "rejoice and be glad and give Him glory, the wedding of the Lamb has come and His Bride has made herself ready. Fine linen, bright and clean, was given to her to wear, and fine linen stands for the righteous acts of the saints. And the angel said to me, write, 'Blessed are those who are invited to the wedding supper of the Lamb'" (Rev. 19:7–9).

True Anointing

There's something else that will determine whether you can stand before God and enter into His Banquet Table of Eternity. Matthew 25 is a dire warning. Ten *virgins* are waiting for the Bridegroom. Understand this, these are "virgins." Five were foolish. They thought because they had kept themselves pure, they could still enter the door of this festive banquet. Some will always try to do "the right things" by the world's standards. But they're dead wrong! When the sound came that the bridegroom was coming, those five had allowed their lamps to grow dim. They didn't have much passion, no real longing to see the Bridegroom as noted by their unpreparedness, just like the man at the wedding feast Jesus was speaking about.

Little did they know their lights were about to fizzle, fade, and go out forever. This is Revelation 3:16 to be sure. There is no room at this eternal marriage table for the ignorant lukewarm. In desperation, these five virgins began crying out, "'Lord, Lord, open up for us.' But he answered and said, 'Truly I say to you, I do not know you'" (Rev. 3:16). You must know the Lord for yourself and not try to squeeze through the doors of eternity on someone else's anointing. Get the oil and fire yourself. Make time to read the Word of God for yourself. Don't be lazy! Pay the price! It will pay endless dividends.

We must realize that even one of the Lord's closest apostles, Philip, who was in the inner circle of the twelve, was cautioned by Jesus, "Have I been so long with you, and yet you have not come to know Me, Philip?" (John 14:9). Many who have gone to church for years fall into this category. They really don't know Jesus personally.

Some don't even care about His Jewish roots! Each of us must become intimately acquainted with the heart of the Savior. He is coming back for His faithful Bride, not some redesigned or reassigned version of her. Nor is He coming for a bridegroom. He's after a holy bride, one who is pure, guarding her covenantal relationship with her King of glory with passionate desire for Him (Eph. 5:27).

He's coming! He's coming! Do you hear the horses?

Prayer

Holy Spirit, open my eyes to see the good things You have planned for me. Clothe me in Your righteousness and prepare my heart with oil from Your Throne Room. I want to be ready for Your Second Coming! Amen.

◆ sixteen ◆

THE ENGRAVED WEDDING INVITATION

GOING TO THE mailbox and receiving an invitation to some important event makes one feel good. Perhaps the reason is we know we haven't been left out! I know I felt that way when we got an invitation to a presidential candidates' gathering. It's exciting to get important invitations.

How much more so when it's from the King of kings! He has been sending out holy invitations to His banqueting table for millennia. "He has brought me to His banquet hall and His banner over me is love" (Song of Songs 2:4). The Father's call to the Bridal Banquet of His Son Jesus will not be with a little tinkling bell. It will be with the blast of a trumpet! It will be the final trumpet call for all mankind, and it will be the end of the beginning…the beginning of Christ's one thousand-year-reign on earth (Rev. 20). The trumpet of God is the most significant sound the world will ever know. It will be clarion, distinct and utterly loud—so loud, in fact, that it will fill the earth. Can you even begin to imagine the power of a sound that piercing? It is coming! We must be ready. It cannot be otherwise, for our very lives depend upon it.

The apostle Paul writes in 1 Corinthians 15:51–52, "Behold, I tell you a mystery: We shall not all sleep, but we shall all be changed—in a moment, in the twinkling of an eye, at the last trumpet. For the trumpet will sound, and the dead will be raised incorruptible, and we shall be changed." What shock, awe, and terror will fill the earth. What holy reverential fear of God that will bring.

This event is most commonly referred to as the Rapture. It's a holy capture! Those who have passionately pursued their heavenly Bridegroom, Jesus, will be captured by His love, power, and glory forevermore. Are you aware that this shocking trumpet blast will signal the last of human civilization as we know it?

Wise Noah

The book of Revelation is the last book of the Bible yet to be lived and experienced. There will be a generation to do so. Will it be ours, our children, grandchildren, great-grandchildren, or great-great grandchildren? No one knows (Luke 12:40). But the certainty is that there will indeed be a final trumpet call. So we *all* need to be ready on a moment's notice, prepared for instant departure! In the meantime, life does go on—day by day, week by week, month by month, and year by year. However, the sands of time are sifting toward that ultimate moment and we must not miss it as some did when Noah was building the Ark. The Bible says, "For as in those days which were before the flood they were eating and drinking, they were marrying and giving in marriage, until the day that Noah entered the ark, and they did not understand until the flood came and took them all away, so shall the coming of the Son of Man be" (Matt. 24:38–39). How sad that multitudes were lost in the flood waters because they would not listen to Noah. They chose not to prepare for an impending disaster that seemed incomprehensible. But, "by faith Noah, being warned by God about things not yet seen, in reverence prepared an ark for the salvation of his household, by which he condemned the world, and became an heir of the righteousness which is according to faith" (Heb. 11:7). Faith in the utterances of God will keep us alive in His Presence for eternity.

History tends to repeat itself. Just as it was in Noah's day, that final generation will be likewise. Human nature has not changed, unless of course, one decides to live by the power of the Holy Spirit. And the Holy Spirit will quicken His people to stay alert and live by higher standards than those of the world. He will caution them to stay on red alert and to abide without fear in the power of the blood of Calvary. He will bear witness in their hearts to the Truth of the Lamb of God and the power of the Cross that saves! But woe to those who are still eating and drinking and marrying and giving in marriage without regard to the laws of God and His heart. Psalm 29:10 says, "The Lord sat as King at the flood; yes, the Lord sits as King forever."

Stay watchful. God is faithful to perform His Word (Isa. 55:11).

The Abomination

"And I saw the holy city, new Jerusalem, coming down out of heaven from God, made ready as a bride adorned for her husband" (Rev. 21:2). Friends of the Bridegroom, when that last trumpet shall sound, we'll know the heavenly, eternal wedding is about to begin. The engraved invitations, set in stone by the Rock of Ages, have been sealed and delivered through the

Word of God for millennia and by the consummation of the blood contract of Calvary. Jesus, the heavenly Bridegroom, appears on His brilliant and glorious white horse looking like the Knight in shining armor that He is, and looks around for His beautiful bride (Rev. 19:11–14). His Presence breaks the eastern skies over Israel and all eyes behold His glory. Our Jewish wedding commences!

It's not surprising that satan wants to defy and desecrate the bridal city of Jerusalem! One of those avenues is by using the event of gays, lesbians, bisexuals, and trans-genders called World Pride. They're encroaching upon this holy city. Their event is aptly named. Pride, of course, was satan's downfall. He chose his own self-will over God's will. Time and time again this demon says in Isaiah 14, "I will…I will…I will…" One needs only to look into the very breath of God in scripture and read the truth concerning these defilements. First John 2:16–17 says, "For all that is in the world, the lust of the flesh and the lust of the eyes and the boastful pride of life, is not from the Father, but is from the world. And the world is passing away, and also its lusts; but the one who does the will of God abides forever." Pride is a sure killer! Let us all repent of our varied sins under the grace of God while there's still time.

Examine this a moment. Could this World Pride event that's invading the Holy Land be the "abomination of desolation" spoken of in Matthew 24:15? (See also Dan. 9:27; 11:31; 12:11.) We know from God's Word that believers in *Yeshua* (Jesus) are called "living stones," and our inheritance lies within those sacred streets of Jerusalem (1 Pet. 2:5; 2 Cor. 6:14–18). Jesus has made us to be a living tabernacle of God where

Immanuel dwells within. But we must take to heart the passage in Revelation 21:27, "And nothing unclean and no one who practices abomination and lying, shall ever come into it, but only those whose names are written in the Lamb's book of life"; and also 22:15, "Outside are the dogs and the sorcerers and the immoral persons and the murderers and the idolaters, and everyone who loves and practices lying." These immoral events held in Jerusalem very well may be the signal of desolation! If this is the case, this would hasten Armageddon and the fight for the true bride.

May there be a trembling upon our very souls! Why test this? Why tempt God? Every one of us needs to bend our knees to the Lord, repenting of all our sins so we can confidently accept His divine wedding invitation and partake of the eternal banquet.

Proper Protocol

All the ages have been in preparation for this moment, "I go to prepare a place for you," says our heavenly Bridegroom, Jesus, in John 14:2. Whether we're aware or not, our Christian lives closely follow Jewish protocol. Jewish tradition required that the bridegroom would go to the house of his fiancée who had been chosen by his parents. This is true spiritually. We have been selected by God the Father, but must accept His invitation. "No one comes to the Father except by the Spirit" (John 6:44).

This Jewish young man would then consult with the girl's father by giving him the customary dowry of those days, which might consist of camels, silver bracelets or whatever else he had to offer. If the price was agreed upon, then the scribe would draw up a *ketubah* or "marriage contract." In today's society, it's the engagement ring that speaks of this promise to marry.

This *ketubah* is what Joseph had in his possession when the Holy Spirit overshadowed Mary as she was indwelt through the *breath* or *Word* of God, and the Word became flesh, and dwelt among us (John 1)! Joseph looked to divorce her because of the serious stigma this young, pregnant woman now carried. But Joseph was a godly man of great insight and wisdom who heeded God's guidance delivered through an angel (Matt. 1:19–20). The church does not give him enough honor for his incredible obedience to the plan of God. Thank goodness he didn't forsake Mary. He walked out his divine destiny with dignity and honor. Hallelujah!

The custom of that time was that the newly engaged bridegroom would take this *ketubah*, return to his father, and begin building a house for himself and his future bride. The marriage ceremony itself could not take place until his father gave full and final approval to the home's specifications and completion. Then he would return to get his betrothed (promised) bride. He would also begin to prepare the wedding canopy where the marriage actually took place.

Simultaneously, the bride would begin preparations as well by daily using special cleansing oils and perfumes. The bride did not know when her bridegroom would return for her. Often, she kept a lamp burning and an extra jar of oil on hand just in case he would come in the evening hours or at night. She was so excited and wanted to make sure she was prepared. Who wants to be caught off guard at a time like that?

How many of us have had to drop everything and run somewhere only to discover how unprepared we were?

Some Haven't Got a Clue!

Unfortunately, this state of being totally unprepared is where many people are spiritually. They haven't got a clue that the trumpet is about to sound. Remember the story of the ten virgins in Matthew 25? Those who are not ready will lose out. What an eternally costly mistake. But those who heed the Savior's invitation, staying in preparedness, will find the door of eternity opened to them for the greatest love feast ever known! "And the Lord of hosts will prepare a lavish banquet for all peoples on this mountain; a banquet of aged wine, choice pieces with marrow, and refined, aged wine" (Isa. 25:6).

Examining further the ancient Jewish tradition of marriage, when the groom's father decided everything was ready, he would release his son to go get his bride. His bride was not a man, not a transsexual, not a transgendered person; she was a woman.

It's significantly beautiful that the first miracle Jesus performed on earth was at a Jewish wedding between a man and a woman. He turned water into wine (John 6). Those whose hearts are soaked in true worship to the Lord will find their miracles. They will find their true identity in Him. For from His bridegroom body flowed blood and water (John 19:34). We are washed and cleansed by the Living Water and sacrificial blood. This first miracle of the Lord solidified the union God ordained for marriage since the foundation of the world. What God has joined together, let not man put asunder (Mark 10:6–9)! What a celebratory and prophetic act

Jesus performed to indicate His Second Coming to take His bride away!

Jewish Custom

In Jewish custom, the son would wait for the father's signal for him to call for his betrothed. When the father gave approval, the son would gather family and friends and begin blowing shofars while dancing and celebrating with great revelry as he went to get his bride. What an exciting sound! It could be heard all over! The bride would hear the sound of his coming. Her heart would beat heavily within her, almost leaping out of her chest. What joyful expectation filled her soul! Songs of happiness flooded her heart, and with tears welling up inside her expectant eyes, she would behold him whom she'd longed for and prepared for.

The protocol was that the betrothed couple would then dance together all the way back to the father's house accompanied by all the joyful participants. The father would be waiting and he would put the hand of his son into the hand of his bride, he would then display the couple to all who had gathered and this would be the moment of *announcement*. After this *presentation*, as it was called, they became husband and wife. The bridegroom would then escort his bride into the bridal chamber that had been prepared by the approval of the father.

Have you and I been approved? We need to look very closely at our own *presentation* that it does not bring offense to our heavenly Father.

The Heavenly Bridegroom

Our heavenly bridegroom is coming soon to take us away to be with Him forever. He is longing for us as we're longing for Him! But He must wait for the nod from the Father (Mark 13:32). While the church waits, we have great confidence in knowing we have been betrothed to Him in righteousness and purity. We have a great sense of belonging and longing within our souls for our Beloved. The Word says in 2 Corinthians 11:2, "For I am jealous for you with a godly jealousy. For I have betrothed you to one husband, that I may present you as a chaste virgin to Christ."

Unlike today, in biblical times the marriage feast was a celebration to honor the bridegroom, not the bride. This journey of life that we are living isn't so much about us. But it has everything to do with our Eternal Bridegroom. We are not the focus of the universe. Jesus is!

It's not about us. It's about Him. It's about Him receiving all the glory, honor, and praise that is due His magnificent Name. That one, great, spectacular Name! That holy Name which is above all names (Phil. 2:9). Just as an earthly bride takes on her husband's name, so too the Bride of Christ takes His Name and she will be known by that Name forever in blessings beyond belief. It's not like earthly marital vows of "in sickness or in health, or for richer or for poorer," because with this name, there will be no sickness, no sorrow, no tears, no pain (Rev. 21). She will only know bliss forever. "Thou wilt make known to me the path of life; in Thy Presence is fullness of joy; in Thy right hand there are pleasures forever" (Ps. 16:11).

Do you desire this? Do you want to know Him who has loved you before you were ever born? Why not say yes to Him right now? Why not give your heart to Him at this very moment and make your reservation at the Marriage Banquet and the Divine Reception? Pray in your own words. He will hear you. He will come!

Communion

Weddings are beautiful! It's so much fun to go and experience all the joy of everyone gathered. In western culture one of the best parts at the reception is when the couple cuts the cake and has a wedding toast. Usually the best man gives the toast and then others may join in. Friends of the Bridegroom, we must realize every time we take Holy Communion it is a display of our vows to Jesus. We, the Bride of Christ, the body of believers, publicly declare that we are betrothed to Him. This is His holy covenant with us. Sometimes, in my private devotional times with the Lord while taking Communion, I'll raise my cup in a toast to Him! This is a sacred gesture honoring my Beloved who died for me.

Communion is commemoration and consummation that we belong to Jesus. Do you remember His passionate words of His last night on earth? "I have desired to eat this Passover with you before I suffer; for I say to you, I shall never again eat it until it is fulfilled in the kingdom of God…Take this and share it among yourselves; for I say to you, I will not drink of the fruit of the vine from now on until the kingdom of God comes…This is My body which is given for you; do this in remembrance of Me…This cup which is poured out for you is the new covenant in My blood" (Luke 22:15–20).

The new covenant was being initiated by the Savior's own blood which purchased our access into the Holy of Holies. His torture bought the rights for us to go in behind the veil, to go through that membrane that separates the natural from the spiritual. A new order of the day meant those of clean hearts and clean hands, those who repented and accepted the Lamb's bloody sacrifice, could now obtain immediate access into intimacy with God (Rev. 22). It's reserved only for those whose hearts are aligned in a holy covenant with the heavenly Bridegroom. Dear people, let us not abuse and defy this holy covenant by accepting the world's view of the marriage covenant that God the Father has divinely put into place.

Your Hope Chest

In our culture, it used to be that girls had a hope chest. Oftentimes it was a wooden chest made out of cedar, and it was where they stored up things for their wedding day. This closely resembles a verse from the intimate book of Song of Songs, "The beams of our houses are cedars, our rafters, cypresses" (1:17). Jesus, our Bridegroom, built an eternal home through a wooden tree called Calvary for His bride, the church. There are many treasures stored up for us there!

What's in *your* hope chest? What's in your heart? Is it empty? Does your heart beat with passionate desire for the Lover of your soul? Have you prepared for the trumpet call? Even though no one knows when that final breath in his or her bodily chest will depart, we can know assuredly we'll be with our eternal Bridegroom forever. It's a matter of taking His Name and applying it to our hearts.

Eternity is a timeless realm where every created soul will live. There are multitudes within God's holy Presence in heaven. And there are multitudes in hell without

His Presence. No one knows when that last blast of the trumpet will sound, but we can be fully dressed and prepared to leave! We need to have our spiritual suitcase—our hearts—packed with the Lord's saving grace. Out of a reverential fear of God, Noah prepared an Ark against all odds (Heb. 11:7). He didn't have a gambling bone in his body. But to those with wicked and unbelieving hearts, he looked like a fool. Noah clung to his faith in God. He knew that what the Almighty says, He does! "God is not a man that He should lie, nor a son of man, that He should repent; has He said, and will He not do it? Or has He spoken, and will He not make it good?" (Num. 23:19).

Let us accept the invitation to enter the Ark of salvation in Jesus. Let us accept His divine dinner invitation for the Bridal Banquet. Our *hope chest* of love has prepared us in purity for our eternal covenant of spiritual marriage. Come, O people of God, let us proclaim the true, holy reverential fear of the Lord because what He says, He does! He's coming a second time, truly He is!

"He who testifies of these things says, 'Yes, I am coming quickly.' Amen. Come Lord Jesus" (Rev. 22:20).

Prayer

Lord, I accept Your divine wedding invitation! I vow to prepare myself with proper wedding garments of righteousness through Your saving blood. I will partake of Holy Communion in a new dimension than ever before because I know it's an encounter with You. I adore and worship You forever. Amen.

◆ seventeen ◆

PROPHETIC BRIDAL SHOWERS

IF YOU'VE EVER planned a wedding, you know there's much to do! There is a vast array of things to be done in preparation for the big day. The details seem to be endless and can begin to cause stress. But there's always that anticipation for what is about to come, that causes you to keep moving forward toward that special time. I've discovered that even so-called professional wedding planners can make a lot of mistakes. This actually happened at one of our daughters' weddings. Some things you just have to do yourself!

My friends, spiritually speaking, it's no different when planning for the Eternal Wedding with our heavenly Bridegroom, Jesus. If we're going to rely strictly on professional clergy to get us there, forget it. It just won't happen. *You* have to do it yourself! No one can take you to heaven on their coattails. You can learn much from many anointed teachers and preachers, but you're going to have to know the Lord for yourself. You've got to know Him up close and personal. You've got to know the sound of His voice, "To him the doorkeeper opens, and the sheep hear his voice, and he calls his own sheep by name and leads them out. When he puts forth all his own, he goes before them, and the sheep follow him because they know his voice" (John

10:3–4). You've got to know His likes and dislikes. All this "knowing" gives you influence and power.

The Father of the Bride loves His precious child very much. He can't wait to sound the trumpet, heralding her walk down the aisle of golden streets in heaven! You, the bride, the Church of Jesus Christ, can plan your own entrance! However, as life often spins around furiously, we all know some days are harder than others. In fact, some are so difficult at times you just want to give up. Jesus said in this life we will have trials, heartaches, and tribulations, but we should actually rejoice because through Him we are victorious (John 16:33). Keeping our eyes on the big day and its spectacular rewards is worth all the effort.

An Invitation

There is an invitation from the Lord in Revelation 3:20 which says, "Behold, I stand at the door and knock; if anyone hears My voice and opens the door, I will come in to him, and will dine with him and he with Me." What a dinner party! As most us know, a part of most weddings is the rehearsal dinner. At that point, you know the wedding is at hand! Church, *this is where we are in history.* We are in the rehearsal stages for the Big Day! People all over the globe are having a sense of things changing dramatically. However, many can't pinpoint what it is. I believe what they're feeling is the final movements for the coming of Christ. Souls everywhere sense the stage is being set for something of great magnitude to occur. Could it be the final battle for the bride?

Bridal Showers

There was a season when God called our ministry to have several "bridal showers" for the Lord. In the same way an earthly bride and bridegroom (in western culture) have bridal showers before their wedding to prepare for their new life together, so too should the body of Christ. It's a clear signal that the couple is getting ready for a lifestyle change. It will no longer be about one or the other of them, but about their lives together in the bond of a holy covenantal love. So it is spiritually. So our ministry gathered together the body of Christ as the Lord directed, having four specific mandates.

The first one was repentance. We needed to get cleaned up! We needed to be washed and purified by the Blood of the Lamb of God. Our heavenly Bridegroom asks for His beautiful bride (the church) to be holy, "that He might present to Himself the church in all her glory, having no spot or wrinkle or any such thing; but that she would be holy and blameless" (Eph. 5:27). We confessed our own sins, but also the sins of our nation. We prayed regarding generational curses that may have plagued families for years. Does any of this resound in your spirit? Is this something you need to pray as well? Needless to say, cleansing is good for the soul. Burdens are placed on the cross and lifted, ushering in freedom and refreshment of soul. This brings access to the other side of the Cross where Resurrection power is released! Do you want that? If you fall on your knees with repentance pouring from your heart, you'll feel so much better as the power of Christ comes in!

The Ring of Fire

The second thing we did was to pray for Israel as the first fruits of intercession according to Psalm 122:6, "Pray for the peace of Jerusalem. May those who love you prosper." The Bride of Christ must learn that unless our hearts are knit together with Israel, there can be no significant or lasting fruit. We need her and she needs us! This is a divine mandate from the Word of the Lord as seen in this Psalm. We need to live it and act upon it. There is no hidden meaning. It is as it says. Therefore, if any one of us is looking to prosper we might take this verse more seriously.

Is it any wonder that much of the church today struggles so much? Program after program may prosper for a season, but in the end, if there is no heart for Israel, it will be pruned because there has to be room in our hearts for God's chosen people of which we've been so beautifully grafted in. Dear church, if we would carry this mandate of prayer for Israel, this passage from Isaiah 49:18–19 would manifest: "Lift up your eyes and look around; all of them gather together, they come to you. As I live, declares the Lord, you shall surely put on all of them as jewels and bind them on as a bride. For your waste and desolate places, and your destroyed land—surely now you will be too cramped for the inhabitants….You shall surely put on all of them as jewels and bind them on as a bride." You just might see revival!

If you want to be a bride of the Lord Jesus, you will have to love Israel because she is God's crowning jewel. This passage states that Israel's former devastators will come bowing before her. War is coming. It's inevitable as the end of the age draws near. Whose side will you be on?

We could be blessed so much more if our Jewish roots were addressed more often in the church. "For I am not ashamed of the gospel, for it is the power of God for salvation to everyone who believes, to the Jew first and also to the Greek. There will be tribulation and distress for every soul of man who does evil, of the Jew first and also the Greek, but glory and honor and peace to every man who does good, to the Jew first and also to the Greek" (Rom. 1:16; 2: 9–10; also read Rom. 9; 11:25–27).

Because Israel is likened to a bride by the Lord, the passage in Zechariah 2:4–5 is very exciting indeed. It's as though Jerusalem is the fiery, golden wedding ring! "Run, speak to that young man, saying, 'Jerusalem will be inhabited without walls, because of the multitude of men and cattle within it.' 'For I,' declares the Lord, 'will be a wall of fire around her, and I will be the glory in her midst.'" Let those who stand with her, stand now. Let us be witnesses at this holy wedding that's about to transpire.

Prophetic Declarations

The third thing we did at our bridal showers for the Lord was make declarations and decrees for the fulfillment of past and present prophecies that have been spoken regarding Israel, the body of believers worldwide and regionally. In the book of Esther, after becoming the bride of the King, Esther is able to have great influence with him. In light of that, at her request, the king makes decrees in His name to save her entire nation! The bride has power because she carries the name of the Bridegroom! Do you have power or do you feel powerless? Check your pulse. See if your heart is beating for yourself or for the King. Therein lies your answer to whether you have power or not.

Esther had to go through many preparations in order to go in to the King. She also wisely took counsel from her uncle Mordecai. Watch for your own Mordecai. Watch for those godly people who have influence in your life who give words of encouragement or prophecy declaring, "Who knows whether you have not attained royalty for a time such as this?" (Esther 4:14).

The fourth and final thing we did at these amazing events was to have an intimate, candlelit time of Holy Communion. This was always the highlight of the whole event! The Bride of Christ participates in a depth of communication or communion with Him that goes behind the veil to an ever-deepening degree. "But we all, with unveiled face beholding as in a mirror the glory of the Lord, are being transformed into the same image from glory to glory, just as from the Lord, the Spirit" (2 Cor. 3:18). As the bride enters into that realm of glory in the King's heart, as she hungers for His Presence, she's taken from glory to glory. It's an inexhaustible realm! Do you know this kind of communion? If not, isn't it time to pursue the Lover of your soul with a new passion and desire that will transcend anything you've ever known? Let the King escort you from chamber to chamber and from glory to glory inside His holy heart of love.

A Dream

I had a dream one night while writing this chapter of the book. It was a brief one. In the dream, it seemed as if it were night as everything was dark. It was as though I were backtracking, or trying to find my way back somewhere (home?) in order to find a safe haven. I came across a drawbridge or swinging-type bridge. It hung over a deep chasm! Oddly, as I attempted to cross this bridge, I kept trying to pick up old cameras and camera equipment, cases, and such. Suddenly a voice came from nowhere, "Leave it behind!" Then I saw that my husband, Michael, was on the other end of the drawbridge with his arms stretched out to grab hold of me and draw me to safety. Philippians 3:13–14 is a drawbridge for us when it says, "But one thing I do: forgetting what lies behind and reaching forward to what lies ahead, I press on toward the goal for the prize of the upward call of God in Christ Jesus." (See also Isaiah 43:18–19.)

The next morning, as is my custom, I asked the Holy Spirit to interpret the dream. Dreams are often used by God to either foretell an event or a warning. I felt this dream was both. I sensed the Holy Spirit say that the "old camera" stuff represented some of the old tired-out programs of the church. They were good in their time, but it's a whole new hour! There are times when we may be seeing things through a clouded, old lens, when God wants to give clear vision for what He's doing *now*.

It's not about programs, it's about *relationship* and that's where the emphasis must be, as noted by my own husband in the dream. Our heavenly Bridegroom is standing before us, waiting with open arms to embrace us in intimacy with Him. If we'll do that, we'll cross that deep chasm, and all those attacks from the enemy, and have victory in Jesus!

This dream also represents the church (or a believer) standing on a chasm, precariously perched, swaying between two worlds, that of God and that of man. But we're all being called to cross over into the safety of God's kingdom. (See Luke 16:26.) The dark night represents persecution of the followers of Jesus Christ. It will be a matter of trust to keep crossing that swinging bridge! But we must keep moving forward. To go back is treacherous and extremely dangerous. Who wants to sway back and forth over a dark chasm indefinitely?

The cameras "see" in the past. It's history! Old, tired, worn-out programs and paradigms will pass away as the new hour of the church emerges in all her glory, a bride prepared without spot or wrinkle. It may look dark, but God's people will arise and shine in that hour. Then we shall see Isaiah 60:1–3 manifest, "Arise and shine; for your light has come, and the glory of the Lord has risen upon you. For behold, darkness will cover the earth, and deep darkness the peoples; but the Lord will rise upon you. And nations will come to your light and kings to the brightness of your rising."

THE POINT

I believe the Lord really wants us to get this point about tired-out programs in the church. Ironically, I also had another dream that fit this scenario. In this one, I found myself in a skyscraper in a big city. I was on the ninety-ninth floor and it was dark because it was unlit. It seemed more like a storage room and there were all kinds of religious artifacts in it—crosses, statues, and robes. There were cobwebs on everything.

I felt very sad in the dream, as if something had been lost. Again, I feel the interpretation is the same as the previous one. The Lord also told me the ninety-ninth floor represents how He's after a relationship with each individual. It's not the programs so much that bring people into the kingdom, it's intimacy with Him. "What man among you if he has a hundred sheep and has lost one of them, does not leave the ninety-nine in the open pasture, and go after the one which is lost, until he finds it? I tell you that in the same way, there will be more joy in heaven over one sinner who repents, than over ninety-nine righteous persons who need no repentance" (Luke 15:4, 7). The Lord tells us He is the door of the sheep. Let us pass through the door for more Son Light and fresh insight (John 10:7)!

People, get up! Take action. Arise. Arise to new heights in God, as shown by the "high-rise" building in the dream. Wake up! Shake yourself loose through the Blood of Jesus from the bondages that have held you back, held you down, held you captive, and held back your divine destiny! Get out of your wilderness now! A voice is calling! Do you hear it? "A voice is calling, 'Clear the way for the Lord in the wilderness; make smooth in the desert a highway for our God'" (Isa. 40:1; Matt. 3:3; Mark 1:3; Luke 3:4; John 1:23).

Prepare. Prepare the way of the Lord, for the Love of the Ages is upon us. The rehearsal dinner is *now*!

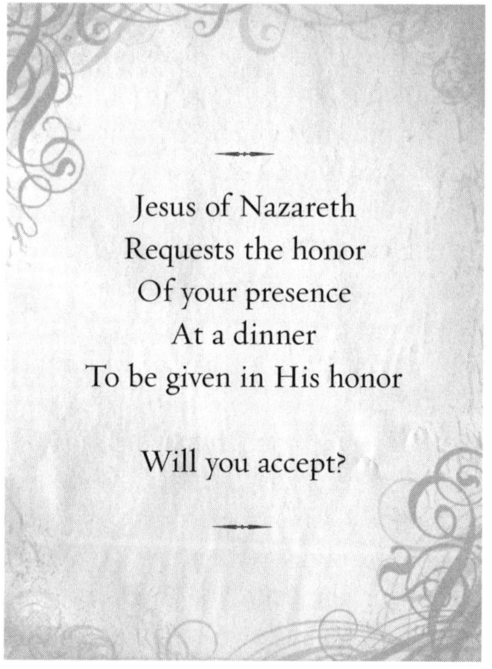

PRAYER

Blessed Lord Jesus, I am excited about Your dinner plans. I accept! And I'm going to walk right into Your arms with complete abandon for a fresh, vibrant walk with You. Amen.

◆ eighteen ◆

THE WEDDING

THERE'S GREAT EXCITEMENT in the air! The day has arrived. Your heart throbs with excitement. Your joy is rapturous. It's your day—your wedding day. You've lived all your life for this moment!

As people begin to gather, you realize all the preparations have been worth it. Your passionate longing gives way to reality.

Dear friends of the Bridegroom, just as there is great anticipation at an earthly wedding, so it is for our eternal wedding, even more so! Nothing can compare to that grand and glorious moment of rapture with the King of glory!

When our friends and relatives gather together for our weddings on earth, it's an allegory of our spiritual one. When Jesus comes, the Redeemed of the Lord will be there (Isa. 35:8–10)! They'll be from every tribe, tongue, and nation (Rev. 5:9). Just think of it. The wedding hall will be filled to overflowing as far as the eye can see. Armageddon will have passed away with judgments rendered, and the eternal celebration will begin!

Runaway Bride

There will be much that transpires in our hearts leading up to that moment in time. Most of us have heard stories of either the bride or groom not showing up for their own wedding. It's sad and it devastates the family and their circle of friends. It denotes a shaky commitment on the part of the one who didn't appear. Perhaps they pondered, "Am I doing the right thing?" and in their fear and doubt, changed their mind. So we need to ask ourselves how committed we are to this relationship with Jesus. Is it shaky or is it on our solid Rock? He is the eternal Rock and one thing is certain with our heavenly Bridegroom, He *will* show up! That day is approaching faster than we can imagine.

The question is, "Will we, the church, be a runaway bride?" Are we going to forsake Him at the altar? Have we been playing church, saying and doing all the outward religious things that make us look good, but inside we're like dead men's bones having no real relationship with the King of glory (Matt. 23:25–28)? Are we really going to make a showing and be all cleaned up, wearing our white garments (Rev. 19:8)? Maybe we ought to think about that. Commitment to Jesus may bring martyrdom. It may not all be a bed of roses, at least, initially. Eternally speaking, however, it most certainly will be because our heavenly Bridegroom is the Rose of Sharon and the Lily of the Valleys (Song of Songs 2:1). What a bridal bouquet!

A Full Heart

We must approach our wedding day with a full heart for our blessed Lord. A halfhearted commitment simply will not do! The reason is because the days ahead for the Bride of Christ will be filled with great testing. It could mean that this worldwide battle for the bride and the world's attempt to redefine marriage will bring about a war between lukewarm hearts and hearts filled with fiery passion for Christ (Rev. 3:16). Remember, it was the religious establishment that put Jesus to death.

There is another thing that will happen at Christ's Second Coming, which is our spiritual wedding day. There will be a terror of the soul that will cause many to flee because they will know they did not live truth. Beloved Paul says in 2 Corinthians 11:2, "For I am jealous for you with a godly jealousy; for I betrothed you to one husband, that to Christ I might present you as a pure virgin. But I am afraid, lest as the serpent deceived Eve by his craftiness, your minds should be led astray from the simplicity and purity of devotion to Christ."

My plea for those reading this is that there would be repentance in your heart now while it is still called today and that you'll make a full commitment to the One who allowed His body to be tortured and ravaged for your sins. The conduit for this is *love*.

Jesus is love incarnate. He loves you so much! But if your love is divided between yourself and the Lord, you will lose in the end. Jesus says, "He who loves his life loses it; and he who hates his life in this world shall keep it to life eternal" (John 12:25). The Bible also brings us this statement, "But now abide in faith, hope, love, these three; but the greatest of these is love" (1 Cor. 13:13). Let the wedding procession begin!

Invitations

Invitations have been sent out well enough in advance for all generations so all the guests can begin to make preparations to attend this grand celebration, "Make ready the way of the Lord. And the Spirit and the bride say, 'Come'" (Matt. 3:3; Rev. 22:17). Will you come? Or will you have excuses? (Matt. 22) Many are called, few are chosen (Matt. 22:14). The chosen are those committed to the Savior at all costs. They have unbridled passion for Him. You see, the heavenly Bridegroom wants to fulfill your heart's desire because He is our all in all! (Col. 3:11). His invitation is exciting!

The Witnesses

Profound joy resides within the heart of the Bride of Christ, the church, as she approaches her wedding day with the Lord. He's coming for her! He's coming soon: "Come here, I shall show you the bride, the wife of the Lamb" (Rev. 21:9). Many in heaven and earth will testify to this holy, unaltered truth. And just as there are "witnesses" to an earthly wedding with the maid of honor and the best man, likewise on that splendid day in glory we will also be surrounded by a "great cloud of witnesses" (Heb. 12:1). These are the ones who have gone before us.

Some of these witnesses have paid a great price to walk with the holy Bridegroom as Hebrews 11 testifies, saying in verse 38 that they were "men of whom the world was not worthy." Let us follow their footprints according to Hebrews 12:1–2, "Therefore, since we have so great a cloud of witnesses surrounding us, let us also lay aside every encumbrance, and the sin which so easily entangles us, and let us run with endurance the race that is set before us, fixing our eyes on Jesus, the author and perfecter of faith, who for the joy set before Him endured the cross, despising the shame, and has sat down at the right hand of the throne of God." There's no mountain too high to keep us from loving Jesus. He is our destiny.

The Guests

Among the most honored guests at a wedding are the parents of the bride and groom. Often, one of the most beautiful moments in the ceremony is when they light the candles or are given a flower. How appropriate. After all, they're the ones who have given much to try to raise their children in the fear and admonition of the Lord, bringing them to this point of maturity physically and spiritually (Eph. 6:4; Prov. 3:11–12; 6:20). But even if this has not been the case, love covers a multitude of sins, and love must prevail (1 Pet. 4:8). God's love in you can cover anyone, at any time. Forgiveness is the key that unlocks the heavens! It cannot be otherwise. Praise God for His heavenly love.

As we walk toward that glorious wedding day of rapture at the end of the age, we must realize the forerunner spirit of Elijah will be evident again, just as it was at the time of John the Baptist (Luke 1:17). Parents and their children will be restored one to another where there has been a breach. The Lord gives us that promise in Malachi 4:5–6, "Behold, I am going to send you Elijah the prophet before the coming of the great and terrible day of the Lord. And he will restore the hearts of the fathers to their children, and the hearts of the children to their fathers, lest I come and smite the land with a curse." It's time to set things straight with our families. Take the time to repent, forgive, and move onward and upward to new heights of glory! Don't be left behind.

Since people from every tribe, tongue, and nation of the earth will be there, we might as well dispense with prejudice right now (Rev. 5:9; 14:6–7). Let's give God glory for all His creative ways of making different people groups. They are just beautiful. They all shine like jewels in His kingdom. He loves all of us. He so loves the people of this entire planet that He gave His only begotten Son for them—every single one (John 10:10). Follow the Lord and you'll find yourself a lover of people. And besides, you've heard the saying, "The more, the merrier." There's plenty of room at the Father's table. No wonder all of heaven was singing a new song in Revelation 5:9. What a party.

Wedding Garments

Shopping for the wedding gown is so fun! All the ladies know this! But like shopping for a car, you can get sticker shock when looking at all the gowns. I remember well the day I called my husband long distance to Des Moines from Pennsylvania where our daughter lived and giving him the price of the dress she had fallen in love with. I think he about fainted. But none of us, our daughter included, had any idea of the prices of these special garments. But it was worth it when we saw her walking down the aisle aglow with love and happiness. It warmed our hearts beyond measure.

Our heavenly Father's desire is to see his sons and daughters extravagantly clothed with purity through the Lamb's blood. This holy blood was the shocking sticker price for you and me to walk down that eternal aisle of glory.

Ecclesiastes 9:8 is interesting, "Let your clothes be white all the time, and let not oil be lacking on your head." We don't have to go around wearing white clothes all the time! But what we are to do is dress and behave in an appropriate manner. Be properly clothed as befitting the King of glory! Irreverent clothing does not exist in God's wardrobe. Luke 12:35–36 is another portion in God's Word that speaks of this crucial manner, "Be dressed in readiness and keep your lamps alight. And be like men who are waiting for their master when he returns from the wedding feast, so that they may immediately open the door to him when he comes and knocks." Are you ready?

Most everyone, when invited to a wedding, comes dressed in their best. The reason is, of course, because of the celebratory nature of the event. One wouldn't show up wearing pajamas or a bathing suit. But that's about how ludicrous our garments often appear to God the Father. He sees the unsaved, as well as those who profess to be His, defying His clothing attire of purity. If we want to dress for success, let's do so in the manner God has ordained for His children. Isaiah 61:10 is lovely, "I will rejoice greatly in the Lord, my soul will exult in my God; for He has clothed me with garments of salvation, He has wrapped me with a robe of righteousness, as a bridegroom decks himself with a garland, and as a bride adorns herself with her jewels." (See also Zechariah 3:5; Revelation 3:5, 18; 7:9.) So put on the garment of praise and have fun (Isa. 61:3).

Selection of the Veil

Many of the aspects of this heavenly wedding would require a book! However, we are only examining these things in light of the context of victorious eschatology. The veil is significant. It's one of the most exquisite pieces for the bride's presentation to her bridegroom and the witnesses gathered. The white veil is thin and transparent. It is a representation of the thin membrane separating the two worlds of the natural and supernatural.

Likewise, until that veil is lifted, the bride does not yet belong to the bridegroom. But, oh the joy when the veil is lifted and the heavenly kiss commences! Often the congregation will applaud that crowning moment.

Ladies and gentlemen, darkness is coming upon the earth to a frightening degree. It will be a darkness that can actually be felt just as it was in Exodus 10 when God used Moses to deliver the Hebrew children from godless Egypt. It will be a natural darkness, but it will also be a reflection of the spiritual darkness in many people's hearts across the globe:

> But their minds were hardened; for until this very day at the reading of the old covenant the same veil remains unlifted because it is removed in Christ. But to this day whenever Moses is read, a veil lies over their heart; but whenever a man turns to the Lord, the veil is taken away. But we all, with unveiled face beholding as in a mirror the glory of the Lord, are being transformed into the same image from glory to glory, just as from the Lord, the Spirit.
>
> —2 Corinthians 3:14–16, 18

As evil takes its place in greater degrees of degradation (Dan. 8), the Living Light of God's glory will rise upon His people and slice through the veil separating the two. Some will see light; some will see darkness, just as they did in Exodus 10. There will be nothing to fear for those whose hearts are bound to the Lord because of His light of glory within (Isa. 60). They will shine like the Son! The bride therefore, will glow with God's glory because of her deep intimacy with God. It reflects Moses in Exodus 34:34–35 when he had to veil his face before the people because of the sacredness of it. But when he went in to the tent of meeting, when He met with God in intimacy, the veil was removed! Glory!

What an astoundingly wonderful thing Jesus did for us! His own torturous blood lifted the veil separating the natural and the spiritual. Now we can come with our eyes fully opened to truth and enter behind the veil into the Holy of Holies. He bought the rights to the living light of holy revelation and eternal salvation. Luke 23:44–45 says, "And it was now about the sixth hour, and darkness fell over the whole land until the ninth hour, the sun being obscured; and the veil of the temple was torn in two. And Jesus, crying out with a loud voice, said, 'Father, into Thy hands I commit My spirit. And having said this, He breathed His last."

Lift that veil!

Shoes

I haven't been to a wedding where the wedding party was barefoot. I suppose if it were a beach wedding that could happen. Nonetheless, as we shopped for just the right shoes to go with our daughter's wedding gown, it became quite an adventure. Of course, this can be spiritualized, because if the truth were known, everything in life is about the Lord. Turning to the only hope we have, God's unfailing Word, Ephesians 6 says that part of our attire is to have our feet fitted with the readiness that comes from the Gospel of peace. Our heavenly Bridegroom declared to us that He is the Prince of Peace. So as we approach this grand day with Him, let our hearts be inscribed with His words, "Peace, be still" (Mark 4:39; Ps. 46:10; John 14:27). There is no storm in life that we can't conquer through the Prince of Peace. Peace He is! And peace we shall have, if we live and move and have our being in Him. Get fitted for your Gospel shoes now and every place the sole of your foot will set will be holy, victorious ground! (Joshua 1:3–5).

DECORATIONS

Every wedding has its unusual or beautiful decorations. Many hire people to bring creativity into the whole scene. But one of the best ways is through flowers that bring a glorious festivity of color and fragrance. Spiritually then, it's fitting for the Bride of Christ to put on the heavenly fragrance found in 2 Corinthians 2:15, "For we are the fragrance of Christ to God among those who are being saved and among those who are perishing; to the one an aroma from death to death, to the other an aroma from life to life." The wedding of the Lamb of God will be odious to those who haven't received Him in Spirit and in Truth. But to those who have, it will be most fragrant and divine. The Lamb's wife, the church, has been given designer perfume. How heavenly can that be?

The fragrance of expensive, spilled perfume over Jesus' head by Mary Magdalene in John 12 is a beautiful picture of extravagant love. She came to Him with complete abandon and the sweet smell of that love filled the room in a tangible way. In response, Sweet Rose of Sharon, the Lily of the Valleys, questioned those in attendance who did not love in this same manner. We must love Him and others like this! Are we a pleasing fragrance to Him? Can we put on our specially designed fragrance of love and spread its aroma to everyone around us? I believe we can!

The Vows

The vows, of course, are what seal the whole thing! When Christ appears during the Second Coming, His body of believers will enter into divine, eternal bliss and eat at the marriage supper of the Lamb (Rev. 22:4; Rev. 9:4). A foretaste of this banquet can be found in Esther 8. Those who have wined and dined at the enemy's table are putting a satanic seal on their own foreheads (Rev. 13). They are the uninvited wedding guests spoken of in Matthew 22 and 25.

The Celebration Music, Songs, and Dancing

After the declaration of the marriage vows, everyone enters into a time of festive celebration. Many weddings celebrate with some kind of music or dancing. It's so much fun! Even those who rarely dance will get involved, relax, and just kick up their feet! The church needs to dance. It's scriptural and it's so freeing (Ps. 149–150). King David was an especially excited dancer! (See 2 Samuel 6:14–16.) Perhaps you've also been to weddings where impromptu singing erupts as guests get with the flow of fun, laughter, and celebration.

Revelation 4 reveals this utterly glorious praise and song in heaven as the angels worship the King of glory day and night. The singing and rejoicing goes on forever and ever because there is so much to celebrate with an endless Godhead of Father, Son, and Holy Spirit. Every time they encircle the throne of God, they see brilliant, new things about Him! They can't help but sing, sing, sing of this glorious splendor!

Beloved, when a man, woman, or child makes the decision to enter into this holy, pure covenant with the Savior of the world, then the dancing really goes up a notch in heaven! Our eternal Bridegroom declares, "I tell you there is joy in the presence of the angels of God over one sinner who repents" (Luke 15:10). So, come. Start singing and dancing. Celebrate.

Jesus personally designed and purchased the invitation to His wedding banquet with His precious blood. The eternal feast is free of charge for all those who've come through Him. Why walk away from a free offer? Walk according to the ways of God in His holy covenant, and you shall eat and drink forevermore with Him in this glorious celebratory feast!

Congratulations!

Now, rejoice. Sing. Dance. Celebrate. Enjoy. Praise Him. Love Him. Worship Him. Adore Him. And give Him all the glory. Hallelujah. Hosanna in the highest.

EPILOGUE

ISN'T SHE BEAUTIFUL? Isn't the bride beautiful? Oh, the magnificence of her beauty in the eyes of her Beloved. Just one glance of her eyes sets the Bridegrooms' heart ablaze! They were destined for one another and shall live together forever in perfect bliss and harmony. Oh, the beauty of the Bride of Christ, His glorious body of believers, the church worldwide. How He loves her! And she adores Him and loves Him!

This is joy unspeakable! This holy, divine union is beyond our human understanding and must be embraced by the power of the Holy Spirit. The longing in every human heart can be filled to heavenly, splendorous degrees! The Lord Jesus, our eternal Bridegroom, is our magnificent obsession. One could never imagine it could be this way!

The voice of the bride is resonating in this hour upon the face of the earth. The wedding day is nearing, and she's keenly attuned to it. Her crescendo of deep and intense longing for Him has ushered in a new age for the church called the bridal age.

NEW WINE

Precious ladies and gentlemen who hold this book in your hands, hear me now. The best spiritual wine and the most glorious celebration that could ever be known by all of humanity is being reserved until now. It's like a fine wine that's held for many years until it ages to perfection, thereby increasing its value. Spiritually speaking, this is the age we are now in. We have entered into the time of fine wine and an epic, apocalyptic move of God.

John 2:10 is the canopy as the Second Coming of Christ edges nearer. The Lord has reserved the best wine, the best outpouring of His Spirit, in this marvelous hour in which we now live. Glory hallelujah! "'The latter glory of this house will be greater than the former,' says the Lord of hosts, 'and in this place I shall give peace, declares the Lord of hosts'" (Hag. 2:9). This is the bridal wine of the end times that closes out one age, ushering in the next. This outpouring of the new wine will bring miracles, healings, signs, and wonders such as not seen since the time of Moses, but I believe it will surpass that era! The Holy Spirit is going to take us out of earthly bondage and into the Promised Land in a blaze of glory we are yet to behold!

The Lord has shown me the new spiritual bridal wine will not be red like His blood, but it will be white, symbolizing the purity of His bride whom He has found to be without spot or wrinkle. What a joy she is to Him! Oh, the depth of His love! The voice of the true Bride of Christ is arising. She is being set apart for a time such as this.

Jesus lifted up the cup on His last night on earth and gave a toast, if you will, by stating, "I will not drink of the fruit of the vine from now on until the kingdom of God comes" (Luke 22:18). But now Thy kingdom, come, Thy will be done on earth as it is in heaven (Matt. 6:10). "And the Lord of hosts will prepare a lavish banquet for all peoples on this mountain; a banquet of aged wine, choice pieces with marrow, and refined, aged wine" (Isa. 15:6). This is the bride's finest hour!

The Son of God, the heavenly Bridegroom, comes with flames of fire in His eyes. He is captivated by the Bride's beauty, purity, fiery passion, and undying love for Him. He is jealous for her. He's longing for the final trumpet sound to come and take her away to be with Him forever. What a love story (Eph. 5:27)! Quoting the only reliable source mankind has, God's breath, His written Word in the Bible, He declares to the last generation on earth:

> I know your deeds, and your love and faith and service and perseverance, and that your deeds of late are greater than at first. But I have this against you, that you tolerate the woman Jezebel who calls herself a prophetess, and she teaches and leads My bondservants astray, so that they commit acts of immorality and eat things sacrificed to idols. And *I gave her time to repent*; and she does not want to repent of her immorality. Behold, I will cast her upon a bed of sickness and those who commit adultery with her into great tribulation, unless they repent of her deeds. And I will kill her children with pestilence; and all the churches will know that I am He who searches the minds and hearts; and I will give to each one of you according to your deeds. But I say to you, the rest who are in Thyatira, who do not hold this teaching, who have not known the deep things of Satan, as they call them—I place no other burden on you. Nevertheless what you have, hold fast until I come. And he who overcomes,

> and he who keeps My deeds until the end, to him I will give authority over the nations...He who has an ear, let him hear what the Spirit says to the churches.
>
> —Revelation 2:19–26, 29

The days coming will be laden with diverse and severe testings such as have never been upon the earth. There will be much hopelessness. But there will also be much hope! Which camp will you be in?

Decide now!

NOTES

Chapter 2
The Dawning of Divine Romance

1. Spiros Zodhiates, *Hebrew-Greek Study Bible, New American Standard* (Chattanooga, TN: AMG Publishers, 1990), s.v. "Ruwach," #7307.

Chapter 4
Winning Back the Bride

1. Spiros Zodhiates, *Hebrew-Greek Study Bible*, s.v. "Haphak," # 2015.

2. Ibid.

Chapter 6
Identity Crisis

1. Kerry Prewill, Robert I. Hamby, and Stephen J. Gulotta, "Your Total Health," NBC and iVillage, http://yourtotalhealth.ivillage.com/blood-pressure (accessed May 5, 2008).

Chapter 8
Confusion

1. Associated Press, "Marriage Redefined in Texas Textbooks," *Des Moines Register*, November 6, 2004.

2. Lynn Campbell, "Fraternity for Gays, Bisexuals Launched at ISU," *Des Moines Register*, December 10, 2004.

3. Associated Press, "Nation's First Public School for Gay Youths Set to Open," *Des Moines Register*, July 29, 2003.

Chapter 9
Destruction or Discernment? Blood Donor?

1. Elijah List.com, CD of the Month, Nov. 2007.

2. Lewis E. Jones, "There Is Power in the Blood," 1899. Public domain.

3. Julia Ward Howe, "Battle Hymn of the Republic," 1861. Public domain.

Chapter 10
God's Word—A Hot Commodity

1. Spiros Zodhiates, *Hebrew-Greek Study Bible*, s.v. "Ruwach," # 7307.

Chapter 12
Intimacy With God

1. Spiros Zodhiates, *Hebrew-Greek Study Bible*, s.v. "Haphak," # 6310.

2. Ibid., margin notes, page 717.

Chapter 13
Code of Conduct

1. Laurence Urdang, ed., *The American Century Dictionary* (New York: Warner Books, 1996).

2. Richard Jerome, "Honey, I'm Gay," *People Magazine*, September 13, 2004. Others stories taken from *The Des Moines Register*, 2004–2007.

TO CONTACT THE AUTHOR

Intimacy With God Ministries
P.O. Box. 1294
Johnston, Iowa 50131-1294

Web site: www.intimacy-with-God.com
E-mail: LindaSchreurs@intimacy-with-God.com